Berlitz
Malaysia

Text by Jack Altman
Updated by Fong Peng Khuan
Editor: Alex Knights
Series Editor: Tony Halliday

Berlitz® POCKET GUIDE

Malaysia

Tenth Edition 2005

NO part of this book may be reproduced, stored in a retrieval system or transmitted in any form or means electronic, mechanical, photocopying, recording or otherwise, without prior written permission from Berlitz Publishing. Brief text quotations with use of photographs are exempted for book review purposes only.

Photography by:
Lam Seng Fatt 13, 17, 42, 49, 51, 55, 57, 96, 97, 105, 107, 147, 153, 162; Jack Altman 9, 20, 29, 46, 56, 59, 60, 62, 66, 67, 73, 74, 83, 86, 95, 108, 122, 137; Nicholas Sumner 15, 78, 139; Ron Corben 34, 117; Walter Imber 23; Hans Höfer 11, 19, 21, 26, 114, 120; Jill Gocher 25, 87; Ingo Jezierski 43, 44, 77, 79, 81, 85, 88; Arthur Teng 119, 141; Joseph Lynch 98; Tourism Malaysia 6, 7, 33, 36, 41, 45, 48, 52, 61, 68, 71, 72, 91, 92, 101, 102, 111, 113, 121, 125, 126, 129, 131, 133, 134, 142, 144, 146, 148, 151, 154, 156, 159, 161, 164; YTL Hotels & Properties 38, 64; Malaysia Airlines 40; Muzium Negara 30
Cover photograph: Superstock/Powerstock

CONTACTING THE EDITORS
Every effort has been made to provide accurate information in this publication, but changes are inevitable. The publisher cannot be responsible for any resulting loss, inconvenience or injury. We would appreciate it if readers would call our attention to any errors or outdated information by contacting Berlitz Publishing, PO Box 7910, London SE1 1WE, England.
Fax: (44) 20 7403 0290;
e-mail: berlitz@apaguide.co.uk
www.berlitzpublishing.com

All Rights Reserved

© 2005 Apa Publications GmbH & Co. Verlag KG, Singapore Branch, Singapore

Printed in Singapore by Insight Print Services (Pte) Ltd, 38 Joo Koon Road, Singapore 628990.
Tel: (65) 6865-1600. Fax: (65) 6861-6438

Berlitz Trademark Reg. U.S. Patent Office and other countries. Marca Registrada

➤ A short trip from KL, the Batu Caves (page 51) are a breathtaking network of underground limestone vaults

A visit to an Iban longhouse (page 123) is an experience not to be missed when travelling in the state of ▲ Sarawak

The national religion of Islam has given rise to spectacular places of worship like the Blue Mosque (page 49) ▼

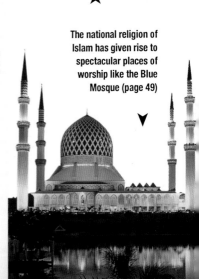

TOP TEN ATTRACTIONS

Gunung Api's pinnacles (page 131) are a spectacular sight in Mulu National Park

◄ Burau Bay (page 93) is one of many beautiful beaches that Langkawi Island has to offer the sun-lover

The world's tallest pair of buidlings, the Petronas Twin Towers (page 45) are a striking sight on Kuala Lumpur's skyline ►

Superb scenery and fascinating flora and fauna make Kinabalu Park (page 136) a major attraction in Sabah ▼

Architecture in George Town (page 79) ranges from colonial to Chinese

Teman Negara (page 64) features rainforests and river rapids ►

Sepilok Orang-Utan Sanctuary (page 142) prepares these once captive animals for life in the wild ►

CONTENTS

Fact Sheets

INTRODUCTION

As Malaysia has moved resolutely into the modern age, it has also remained, culturally and historically, a rich, multi-layered blend of traditions wrapped up in a modern, busy economy. From sandy beaches, broad brown rivers and deep forests, to rising skyscrapers and wide expressways, Malaysia is set to exceed visitors' expectations.

Visitors see the traditional juxtaposed with the modern among Chinatown shophouses, in the vibrancy and aromas of night markets, and even in the modern shopping centres. They see great architectural splendour among the many mosques, the incense-rich Chinese and Hindu shrines, and even the Petronas Twin Towers of Kuala Lumpur. The ways of the past can be lived and felt amid the longhouses of Sabah and Sarawak, in the kite-flying and top-spinning traditions of northeastern Kelantan, in the many graceful and beautiful dance and story-telling traditions, and in the vibrant colours of batik art.

Malaysia offers myriad beautiful beaches and resorts

Your gateway to Malaysia will probably be through its capital, Kuala Lumpur, a prosperous and colourful modern city where stately old mansions, traditional mosques and Hindu temples are squeezed in among expressways and skyscrapers, with green parks and gardens to balance the urban sprawl.

The Petronas Towers, the focal point of Kuala Lumpur City Centre

Situated in the heart of Southeast Asia, Malaysia is about the size of Japan and has a population of over 25 million. The country is divided into two major regions: the peninsula, bordered by Thailand, the Straits of Melaka and the South China Sea; and East Malaysia, whose two provinces, Sabah and Sarawak, are located on the island of Borneo about 800km (500 miles) across the South China Sea. The latter provinces are vast regions of forests, rivers and mountains that border the Indonesian state of Kalimantan and the sultanate of Brunei. Industry and urban society are concentrated on the peninsula, especially on the west coast, while East Malaysia is dominated by the country's characteristic jungle. Malaysia's two regions share a hot, humid climate, but differ greatly in their population density and urban development.

> **Peninsular and East Malaysia together cover a total land surface of 329,759 sq km (127,317 sq miles). The peninsula is 750km (466 miles) long and about 350km (218 miles) at its widest point. It is only two-thirds the size of East Malaysia. Some four-fifths of Malaysia is covered by rainforest. Of the many rivers, the peninsula's longest is the Pahang, at 475km (295 miles). In East Malaysia, the longest river is the Rejang, at 563km (350 miles).**

Malaysia's relative wealth is reflected in the excellent network of roads and a good railway system along the peninsula's west coast. Its per capita income is one of the highest in Southeast Asia, bettered only by that of neighbouring Singapore.

Nature's Supremacy

Whether you are staying at beach resorts or visiting the cities, you will always find the jungle ready to reassert itself. Even in modern, urban Kuala Lumpur, a construction site abandoned too long to the tropical sun and rain will soon sprout a luxuriant growth of *lallang* grass and wild creepers. Water is also a constant presence, sometimes as waves lapping on white sandy beaches, or as beautiful, cascading waterfalls, or as majestic, wide rivers running snake-like across the land.

The country's prosperity has come from its coastal plains, wider on the west than the east side of the peninsula. Malaysia rose first as a trading point for Asia and Europe, with the ports of Melaka (formerly Malacca) and later Singapore, now independent. Then came tin mining and rubber plantations and, more recently, palm oil, hardwood timber and offshore petroleum and gas. Rice paddies in the northwest and around river deltas on the east coast serve only domestic consumption.

Mangrove swamps along the coast and squat nipa palms give rise to mangrove jungle. The world's oldest rainforests engulf low but steeply rising mountain chains that cross the peninsula from east to west like ribs, with one long north–south

Farmers cut terraces in the hillsides to cultivate vegetables and tea

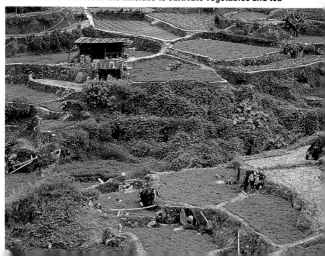

Main Range as their backbone. Until the highway construction of the modern era, access to the jungle interior had been – and sometimes still is – only by river.

In East Malaysia's states of Sarawak and Sabah, on the island of Borneo, plantations alternate with marshland on the coastal plain before giving way to the jungle of the interior. Navigation is hindered by sandbars at the mouth and rapids upriver, though small, sea-going vessels can ply the Rejang in Sarawak and the Kinabatangan in Sabah. To the south, a natural barrier of mountain ranges forms the border with Indonesian Kalimantan. Near the coast at the northern end of the Crocker Range is Mount Kinabalu. At 4,101m (13,455ft), it is the highest peak in Southeast Asia and a climbers' favourite.

Five Kinds of Jungle

Variations in soil, slope and altitude give rise to five kinds of forest:

Mangrove forest. Mangrove trees and shrubs grow on coastal marshland in the brackish zone between the sea and fresh water. A companion is the low, trunkless nipa palm, whose fronds have traditionally been used as roofing material for coastal huts.

Freshwater swamp. Abundant fruit trees in the fertile alluvium of river plains attract prolific wildlife. Where swamp gives way to dry land, you will see the fascinating, monstrous strangler-figs.

Dipterocarp forest. The botanical term refers to the two-winged fruit borne by many of the forest's tallest trees. This dry-land rainforest is what you will see most frequently from just above sea level up to an altitude of 900m (3,000ft).

Heath forest. Poor soil on the flat terrain leading to foothills or on sandy mountain-ridges produces only low, stunted trees with thick leaves.

Montane forest. At 1,200m (4,000ft) and above in large mountain ranges, or as low as 600m (2,000ft) on small isolated mountains, the large trees and liana creepers give way to myrtle, laurel and oak trees.

With the growth of tourism, resort facilities have burgeoned in smaller islands such as Penang, Pangkor and Langkawi on the west coast of the peninsula, Tioman on the east coast, and around Sabah's offshore nature reserve near Kota Kinabalu.

To go to Malaysia without setting foot in the jungle would be to overlook one of the essential beauties of the country. A walk in the jungle is a rare sensual pleasure. Sounds flood in from all sides: the buzz of crickets, the chatter of squirrels, the cries of gibbon apes. You are likely to see everything from the deep gloom of the densest

The mountain forest of Kinabalu

forest to the sudden brilliant burst of sun in a clearing. Animal life may be harder to spot. Unlike the wildlife of the African plain, most animals of the Malaysian jungle are not very conspicuous. Tigers and leopards remain rare, and the elephants, rhinos, tigers and bears of Malaysia are the smallest of their kind. Nevertheless, you are almost bound to see something.

Many and Diverse Peoples

In an era of ethnic conflict, Malaysia can be proud of the continued coexistence of the three most prominent peoples of Asia: Malays (mostly Muslim), Chinese (mostly Buddhist) and Indians (mainly Hindu). Although there has always been the danger of instability, these races generally live in harmony, and it is not extraordinary to see a mosque, pagoda, temple and church all built on the same street. Another result is the marvellous diversity in the national cuisines, with food centres often serving Malay, Chinese and Indian dishes at adjacent stalls. The country's multiculturalism is also apparent in tribal communities like the Kadazandusuns of Sabah, the Iban of Sarawak *(see page 115)*, and the Negritos, a tribe that first arrived on the peninsula at least 10,000 years ago.

> **Courtesy and knowledge of a little Bahasa Malaysia are always welcomed. A simple phrase such as *terima kasih* (thank you) is likely to be answered *sama sama* (you're welcome). Other phrases can be found in the language section *(see page 178)*, but just remembering *selamat pagi* (good morning) or *selamat tengah hari* (good afternoon) is worth the effort, if only for the appreciative smiles you receive.**

The Malays, or *Bumiputra* (meaning sons of the soil), make up over half the population and this is reflected in Islam's status as the national religion, with Malay – *Bahasa Malaysia* – as the national language, Malays benefit from positive discrimination in education and business, as well as almost exclusive access to the principal positions of government at federal and state level. Nevertheless, it is the ethnic Chinese who are the wealthiest community, while the Indians are among the poorest.

At the upper end of the social scale, Malays make up the royal courts of the sultanates. Urban Malays form a modern bourgeoisie, cultivating contacts with the Arab Middle East and keeping only a remote eye on their country estates. The more prosperous send their children to schools overseas.

The bulk of Malays are humbler town- and village-dwelling people, tending goats and buffalo, growing rice, and working in the coconut, rubber, timber, rattan and bamboo industries.

Just as court ritual is still coloured by the ancient customs of pre-Muslim Malaya, so a mild Sunnite version of Islam is often seasoned with the ancient beliefs of animist medicine-men.

Religious Tolerance

To the outsider, public life in Malaysia may sometimes seem like one religious holiday after another. The country is home to all the world's major beliefs, along with an array of minor ones. While Islam is resolutely the official religion, most other faiths are treated with a tolerance that contrasts with ethnic conflicts at the political or economic level. The free pursuit of all beliefs is guaranteed by the constitution. Visitors from abroad may be surprised by the level of devotion among adherents of all faiths; mosques, temples and churches are packed at prayer times and religious observances are performed just as zealously at home.

Cosmopolitan Kuala Lumpur bustles with a unique ethnic mix

Islam is observed by 52 percent of the population, mostly Malays, but also some Indians, Pakistanis and Chinese. First introduced by Arab and Indian Gujarati traders, its earliest trace is an inscribed 14th-century stone found in Terengganu. From 1400, the religion was spread through the peninsula by the Melaka sultanate. Today, each sultan or ruler serves as leader of the faith in his state. Since the world of Islam makes no distinction between secular and religious spheres, it regulates all aspects of everyday life, from greeting people to washing and eating. Visitors need to be aware of Muslim custom and traditions, especially if travelling on the more strict east coast.

Now practised by 17 percent of the population, Buddhism was brought to the peninsula by early Chinese and Indian travellers, but only took hold when Chinese traders came to Melaka in the 15th century. With their 3,500 temples, societies and community organisations, the Chinese practise the Mahayana (Greater Vehicle) form of Buddhism, which evolved in the first century BC. A more rigorous form, known as Hinayana (Lesser Vehicle), is practised by the Thais in the northern states of Kelantan, Kedah and Perlis, the Burmese in and around Penang, and Sri Lankans south of Penang and Kelantan, with headquarters in Kuala Lumpur. For most Malaysian Chinese, the Confucian moral and religious system coexists with Buddhism.

As the country's earliest organised religion, pre-Islamic Hinduism of the Brahman priestly caste reinforced the authority of the Indian ruling class. Relics of that era remain in temple ruins and its rituals survive in Malay weddings and other ceremonies. Modern Hinduism in Malaysia has been shaped by 19th-century immigration from the Indian subcontinent. The largest contingent and most powerful influence were Tamil labourers from southern India and Sri Lanka, with their devotion to Shiva. Temples have been built on almost every plantation worked by Indian labourers. Universal deities are worshipped in the towns.

Malaysia is well known for its diversity of race and religion

Christians make up 8 percent of Malaysia's population, mostly in Sabah and Sarawak. This is largely due to Catholic and Methodist missionary work from the 19th century onwards, although many of the Catholics are of Eurasian origin, dating back to the Portuguese colonisation of Melaka. They keep a relatively low profile, but Christmas is widely celebrated and Easter is a public holiday in Sarawak and Sabah.

Despite its reputation for religious and multiracial harmony, Malaysia faces a constant and serious threat from ethnic instability and extremism. In the political sphere, rifts have deepened between Islamic fundamentalists and more moderate Muslims. Ethnic wealth gaps are also a problem. Nevertheless, Malaysia remains one of Southeast Asia's most successful economies and a top tourist destination. Furthermore, the landslide election victory of the Barisan Nasional party in 2004 has been seen as a clear vote in favour of moderate Islam, continued stability and reform.

A BRIEF HISTORY

Over the centuries, life in Malaysia has always been easy enough to attract a steady stream of immigrants. Bountiful food sources may have made it an inviting place for the contemporaries of Java Man in 230,000BC. But thus far, the country's earliest traces of *homo sapiens,* found in Sarawak's Niah Caves, are fragments of a skull dating to 40,000BC.

By 2,000BC, the nomadic Negrito people, hunting with bows and arrows, were driven back from the coasts by waves of immigrants arriving in outrigger canoes with sails. Mongolians from South China and Polynesian and Malay peoples from the Philippines and the Indonesian islands settled along the rivers of the peninsula and northern Borneo. They practised a slash-and-burn agriculture of yams and millet, a technique that exhausted the soil and imposed a semi-nomadic existence from one jungle clearing to another. Families lived in wooden longhouses like those still seen among the Iban peoples of Sarawak. Other tough migrants from the South Seas settled along the coasts – sailors, fishermen, traders (for the most part pirates) – known euphemistically as *orang laut* (sea people).

Indian Influence

In the early centuries of the Christian era, the peninsula's advantageous position made it an ideal way-station for trade with Bengal and southern India, and attracted Indianised colonies from the Mekong valley of Indochina. Their rulers introduced Buddhist and Hindu culture, Brahmin ministers to govern and an elaborate court ritual. What is now the northern state of Kedah benefited from the plough and other Indian farming practices. From its golden era, a 9th-century Hindu temple, the Candi Bukit Batu Pahat, has been restored on the southern slopes of Mount Jerai. On the east coast in Terengganu and Kelantan, the weaving and metalwork still practised today originate from this early colonisation. So do the region's *wayang kulit* shadow plays inspired by the dramas of the ancient Indian epics, *Ramayana* and *Mahabharata*.

Srivijaya, the most powerful of the Indianised colonies and a centre of Buddhist learning, built a maritime empire from its base on the island of Sumatra. With the *orang laut* pirates as allies, Srivijaya controlled the Straits of Melaka (known in colonial times as Malacca), a key link between the Indian Ocean and the South China Sea. Its colonies on the peninsula's west coast brought with them the Malay language (*Malayu* was the name of a state on Sumatra).

Rice is still harvested using ancient methods of cultivation

As Srivijaya declined in the 14th century, the Malay peninsula was carved up among Siam (now Thailand), Cambodia and the Javanese Hindu empire of Majpahit. Around 1400, fighting over the island of Singapore drove the Srivijaya prince Parameswara to seek refuge up the coast of the peninsula with his *orang laut* pirate friends in their small fishing village of Melaka.

The Glory of Melaka

The Chinese were the first to spot the strategic and commercial potential of Melaka – once an infertile, swampy plain – as a harbour sheltered from the monsoons by neighbouring Sumatra, with a deep-water channel close to the coast. In 1409, under a directive from Emperor Chu Ti to pursue trade in the South Seas and Indian Ocean, a Chinese fleet of 50 ships headed by Admiral Cheng Ho called at Melaka. They made Parameswara an offer he could not refuse: port facilities and financial tribute in exchange for Chinese protection against the marauding Siamese (Thais). In 1411, Parameswara took the money to Beijing himself, and the emperor gratefully made him a vassal king.

Twenty years later, however, the Chinese withdrew from the South Seas trade. The new ruler of Melaka, Sri Maharajah, had switched his allegiance to the Muslim trading fraternity. Islam won its place in Malaya not by conquest, but by trade, dynastic alliances and peaceful preaching. Bengali pedlars had already brought the faith to the east coast. In Melaka, and throughout the peninsula, Islam thrived as a strong, male-dominated religion, offering dynamic leadership and preaching brotherhood and self-reliance – all qualities ideally suited to the coastal trade. At the same time, Sufi mystics synthesised Islamic teaching with local Malay traditions of animistic magic and charisma, though Islam did not become the state religion until Muzaffar Shah became sultan of Melaka (1446–59).

Dog Day Afternoon

According to Malay legend, Prince Parameswara was awakened from his afternoon siesta by the yelping of one of his hunting dogs. The hound had been kicked by a mouse-deer he had been harassing. For some reason, this was felt to be an omen of good luck, so the prince decided to found his new kingdom on the spot and named it after the tree under which he had been sleeping – a malaka. Far-fetched? The less creative and, no doubt, more likely explanation is that the town was named after a nearby island known by an Arab word for market – *malakat*.

Melaka was once a busy trading port

Yet the key figure in the sultanate was Tun Perak, *bendahara* (prime minister) and military commander. He expanded Melaka's power along the west coast and down to Singapore and the neighbouring Bintan islands. He also had *orang laut* pirates patrolling the seas to extort tribute from passing ships. After allied district chiefs had repelled assaults from Siam-controlled armies from Pahang, Tun Perak led a celebrated victory over a Siamese fleet off Batu Pahat in 1456. To smooth things over, the sultan sent a peace mission to the Siamese court and an envoy to China, reconfirming Muzzafar Shah's title as most obedient vassal.

By 1500, Melaka had become the leading port in Southeast Asia, drawing Chinese, Indian, Javanese and Arab merchants away from the hitherto vital port of Pasai in Sumatra. Governed by the great *bendahara* Tun Mutahir with more diplomacy than military force, the sultanate asserted its supremacy over virtually the whole Malay peninsula and across the

Melaka Straits to the east coast of Sumatra. Prosperity was based entirely on the entrepot trade: handling textiles from India, spices from Indonesia, silk and porcelain from China, gold and pepper from Sumatra, camphor from Borneo, sandalwood from Timor and Malay tin from Perak.

Portuguese Conquest

In the 16th century, Melaka fell victim to Portugal's anti-Muslim crusade in the campaign to break the Arab-Venetian domination of commerce between Asia and Europe. The first visit of a Portuguese ship to Melaka in 1509 ended badly, as embittered Gujarati Indian merchants poisoned the atmosphere against the Portuguese. Two years later, the Portuguese sent their fleet, led by Afonso de Albuquerque, to seize Melaka. No match for the Portuguese invaders, the court fled south, establishing a new centre of Malay Muslim power in Johor.

Remnants of the *A Famosa* fort built by Afonso de Albuquerque

Albuquerque built a fort and church on the site of the sultan's palace. He ruled the non-Portuguese community with Malay *kapitan* headmen and the foreigners' *shahbandar* harbour-masters. Relations were better with the merchants from China and India than with the Muslims.

Afonso de Albuquerque

The 130 years of Portuguese control proved precarious. They faced repeated assault from neighbouring Malay forces, and malaria was a constant scourge. Unable or unwilling to court the old vassal Malay states or the *orang laut* pirates to patrol the seas, the new rulers forfeited their predecessors' commercial monopoly in the Melaka Straits and, with it, command of the Moluccas spice trade.

They made little effort, despite the Jesuit presence in Asia, to convert local inhabitants to Christianity or to expand their territory into the interior. They hung on for private profit. The original colony of 600 men intermarried with local women to form a large Eurasian community, served by African slaves and living in elegant luxury – the 'Babylon of the Orient'.

The Dutch Take Over

Intent on capturing a piece of the Portuguese trade in pepper and other spices, the Java-based Dutch allied with the Malays in 1633 to blockade Melaka. The trade blockade was to last eight years, and ended in a seven-month siege. The Portuguese surrendered in 1641, wracked by malaria and dysentery and denied their usual reinforcements from Goa.

The name *Minangkabau* roughly means 'buffalo horns' and is reflected in the distinctive upward curving roofs in museums and government offices built in the Minangkabau style.

By then, the city had become a stagnant backwater.

Unlike the Portuguese, the Dutch decided to do business with the Malays of Johor, who controlled the southern half of the peninsula together with Singapore and the neighbouring Riau islands. Without ever regaining the supremacy of the old Melaka sultanate, Johor had become the strongest Asian power in the region. For the Dutch, Johor provided a buffer against other Europeans. Meanwhile, fresh blood came in with the migration into the southern interior of hardy Minangkabau farmers from Sumatra, while tough Bugis warriors from the east Indonesian Celebes (Sulawesi) roved across the peninsula. The Minangkabau custom of freely electing their leaders provided the model for rulership elections in modern federal Malaysia. Their confederation of states became today's Negeri Sembilan (Nine States), with Seremban as its capital.

The Bugis were energetic merchants and excellent sailors. In the 18th century, with the Dutch concentrating again on Java and the Moluccas, the Bugis took advantage of the vacuum by raiding Perak and Kedah, imposing their chieftains in Selangor and becoming the power behind the throne in Johor.

British Rule

Until the late 18th century, the British had shown little interest in Malaya. That changed in 1786, when the Sultan of Kedah granted Francis Light, a representative of the East India Company, rights to the island of Penang and the strip of mainland coast opposite Province Wellesley (now Seberang Perai) as a counterweight to the demands of the neighbouring Siamese and Burmese. Unlike Portuguese and Dutch trading posts,

Penang was declared a duty-free zone, attracting settlers and traders. An added lure was Light's decision to import large quantities of opium from India. By 1801, the population was over 10,000, concentrated in the island's capital, George Town.

In 1805, a dashing EIC administrator, Thomas Stamford Bingley Raffles, came out to Penang at the age of 24. His knowledge of Malay customs and language, as well as a humanitarian vision for the region's future, made him a vital factor in Britain's expanding role in Malay affairs. Raffles served as lieutenant-governor in Java and Sumatra, but secured his place in history by negotiating, in 1819, the creation of the Singapore trading post with the Sultan of Johor. Singapore became the capital of the Straits Settlements – as the EIC called its Malay holdings, incorporating Penang and Melaka – and was the linchpin of Britain's 150-year presence in the region.

Stamford Raffles

The Straits Settlements were formed after the Anglo-Dutch Treaty of London (1824). This colonial carve-up partitioned the Malay world through the Melaka Straits. The peninsula and Sumatra, after centuries of common language, religion and political, cultural and social traditions, were divided. The islands south of Singapore, including Java and Sumatra, went to the Dutch. Peninsular Malaysia and northwest Borneo remained under the British, but their influence was limited. From 1826, British law was technically in force, but in practice few British people lived in the Straits, and Asian community affairs were run by merchant leaders serving as unofficial *kapitans.*

With the exception of the few Malays in the settlements' rural communities of Province Wellesley and the Melaka hinterland, the majority still lived inland along the middle reaches of the rivers. Unity among them and the east coast communities trading with the Siamese, Indochinese and Chinese came from their shared rice economy, language, Islamic culture, and political and social customs inherited from the Melaka sultanate.

After the painful experience of the American Revolution, the EIC's conducting of business from the islands of Penang and Singapore epitomised the British policy of insulating colonies from local politics. Province Wellesley merely acted as a mainland buffer for Penang, and Melaka similarly turned its back on affairs in the hinterland. When Kedah and Perak sought British help against Siam, the British took the easier option of siding with the Siamese to quell revolts. But in the 1870s, under the Colonial Office, the handsome profits gained from exporting Malayan tin through Singapore forced the British to take a more active role in Malay affairs.

The lucrative tin mines of Kuala Lumpur in the State of Selangor, of Sungai Ujong in Negeri Sembilan, and of Larut and Taiping in Perak were run for the Malay rulers by Chinese managers providing coolie labour. Chinese secret societies waged constant gang wars for the control of the mines, bringing production to a halt at a time when world demand for tin was at a peak. In 1874, Governor Andrew Clarke persuaded the Malay rulers of Perak and Selangor to accept British Residents as advisors in their state affairs. In return, Britain offered protection and mediation in the conflicts.

It began badly. Within a year the Resident in Perak, James Birch, was assassinated after efforts to impose direct British government. Subsequent British advisors served on a consultative state council alongside Malay ruler, chiefs and Chinese *kapitans*. Birch's successor in Perak, Hugh Low (1877–89), was more successful. He spoke Malay, was familiar with local customs and religion, and respected chiefs and peasants alike. Reforms he persuaded the ruler to accept included organising revenue collection, dismantling slavery and regulating land. The peninsula's unity was enhanced by the growing network of railways and roads. Governor Frederick Weld (1880–7) extended the residency system to Negeri Sembilan and the more recalcitrant Pahang, where Sultan Wan Ahmad was forced to open the Kuantan tin mines to British prospectors.

A Federation of Malay States – Selangor, Perak, Negeri Sembilan and Pahang – was proclaimed in 1896 to coordinate

Colonial State Legislative Building at Penang

an economic and administrative organisation. Frank Swetten-ham became first Resident-General of the Federation, with Kuala Lumpur as the capital.

The White Rajahs of Borneo

In the 19th century, Borneo remained relatively undeveloped. Balanini pirates, fervent Muslims, disputed the coast of northeastern Borneo (modern Sabah) with the sultanate of Brunei. Sarawak's coast and jungle interior were controlled by the Iban – Sea Dayak pirates and Land Dayak slash-and-burn farmers. The region's only major resource was the gold and antimony mined by the Chinese in the Sarawak river valley. Brunei chiefs traded the metals through Americans in Singapore.

James Brooke

In 1839, the governor of Singapore sent James Brooke (1803–68) to promote trade links with the Sultan of Brunei. He had been an audacious cavalry officer in the Anglo-Burmese wars and now exploited the situation for his own benefit. In exchange for helping the regent end a revolt on the part of over-assertive Malay chiefs, Brooke was made Rajah of Sarawak in 1841, with his capital in Kuching (founded by the Malays just 11 years earlier). He tried to halt the Dayaks' piracy and head-hunting (believed to bring spiritual energy to their communities), while defending their more 'morally acceptable' customs. His attempts to limit the opium trade met with resistance from the Chinese in Bau, who revolted. His counter-attack with Dayak warriors drove the Chinese out of Bau and across the Sarawak border. Thereafter, Chinese settlement was discouraged and did not achieve the commercial dominance it had on the peninsula.

In 1863, Brooke retired to Britain, handing Sarawak over to his nephew, Charles. More reserved but a better administrator and financier than his uncle, Charles Brooke imposed on his men his own austere, efficient lifestyle. He brought Dayak leaders onto his ruling council but favoured the colonial practice of divide and rule by pitting one tribe against another to keep the peace.

In 1877, northeast Borneo (Sabah) was 'rented' from the Sultan of Brunei by British businessman Alfred Dent, who was operating a royal charter for the British North Borneo Company – a set-up similar to that of the EIC. This region was grouped together with Sarawak and Brunei in 1888 as a British protectorate, North Borneo, but it did not gain the status of a crown colony.

The Early 20th Century

The British extended their control over the peninsula by putting together the whole panoply of colonial administration. At the same time, the tin industry, which had been dominated by Chinese using labour-intensive methods, passed increasingly into the hands of Westerners, who employed the modern technology of gravel pumps and mining dredges. Petroleum had been found in northern Borneo, at Miri, and in Brunei, and the Anglo-Dutch Shell company used Singapore as its regional depot for its oil supplies and exports.

But the major breakthrough for the Malay economy was the triumph of rubber, developed by the director of Singapore

Botanical Gardens, Henry Ridley. World demand increased with the growth of the motor car and electrical industries, and rocketed during World War I. By 1920, Malaya was producing 53 percent of the world's rubber. The Malay ruling class again took a back seat. Together with effective control of the rubber and tin industries, the British now firmly held the reins of government. The sultans were left in charge of local and religious affairs, content with their prestige, prosperity and security.

The census of 1931 was an alarm signal for the Malay national consciousness. Bolstered by an influx of immigrants to meet the rubber and tin booms, non-Malays now slightly outnumbered the indigenous population. The Depression of 1929 stepped up ethnic competition in the shrinking job market, and nationalism developed to safeguard Malay interests against the Chinese and Indians rather than the British imperial authority.

Though hampered by the peninsula's division into the States and the Straits Settlements, relatively conservative Muslim intellectuals and community leaders came together at the Pan-Malayan Malay Congress in Kuala Lumpur in 1939. The following year, they were joined in Singapore by representatives from Sarawak and Brunei. Teachers and journalists urged the revival of the common Malay-Indonesian consciousness, split by the Anglo-Dutch dismemberment of the region in the 19th century. This spirit was a factor in the gathering clouds of war.

Japanese Occupation

The Pacific War actually began on Malaysia's east coast, near Kota Bharu, 70 minutes before the attack on Pearl Harbor. On 8 December 1941, Japanese troops landed from assault vessels on Sabak Beach *(see page 99)*. Japan coveted Malay's natural resources of rubber, tin and oil and the port of Singapore through which they passed. The stated aim of the Japanese invasion was a 'Greater East Asia Co-Prosperity Sphere', appealing to Malay nationalism to throw off the Western imperialist yoke in a movement of Asian solidarity – an 'Asia for the Asians' spearheaded by Japan's Imperial Army.

Not expecting a land attack, Commonwealth troops on the peninsula were ill-prepared. Indian infantry inflicted heavy losses from their bunkers on the beaches but finally succumbed to the onslaught. The landings were launched from bases ceded to the Japanese by Marshal Pétain's French colonial officials in Indochina and were backed by high-performance fighter jets.

Japanese infantry poured in from Thailand to capture airports in Kedah and Kelantan. To counter the Kota Bharu landings two of the British overseas fleet's battleships sailed north. But without air cover, they were spotted off the coast of Kuantan and sunk by Japanese bombers. The Singapore naval base was left empty. Kuala Lumpur fell on 11 January 1942 and, five weeks later, Singapore was captured. Northern Borneo was overrun, but the oil fields of Miri and Brunei were pre-emptively sabotaged by the British and Dutch.

The National Monument in KL

If Japanese treatment of Allied prisoners of war in Malaya was notoriously brutal, the attitude towards Asian civilians was more ambivalent. At first, the Japanese curtailed the privileges of the Malay rulers and forced them to pay homage to the

Japanese leaders surrender their swords in 1945

Japanese Emperor. Then, to gain Malay support, the Japanese upheld their prestige, restored pensions and preserved their authority, at least in Malay customs and Islamic religion.

The Chinese, notably those supporting Mao Tse Tung's combat against the Japanese, were massacred in their thousands. From 1943 Chinese communists led the resistance in the Malayan People's Anti-Japanese Army, aided by the British, to prepare an Allied return.

The Emergency

The Japanese surrender left in place a 7,000-strong resistance army led by Chinese communists. Before disbanding – and stashing weapons in the jungle – the army wrought revenge on Malays who had collaborated with the Japanese. This in turn sparked a brief wave of racial violence between Malays and Chinese, accentuating the ethnic conflicts that would hamper the post-war quest for national independence.

To match their long-term stake in the country's prosperity, the Chinese and Indians wanted political equality with the Malays. Nationalists in the new United Malays National Organisation (UMNO) resented this 'foreign' intrusion imposed by 19th-century economic development. To give the Malays safeguards against economically dominant Chinese and Indians, the British created the new Federation of Malaya in 1948. Strong central government under a High Commissioner left considerable powers in the hands of the states' Malay rulers. Crown colony status was granted to Northern Borneo and Singapore, the latter excluded from the Federation because of its large Chinese majority. The Chinese, considering their loyalty to the Allied cause in World War II, felt betrayed. Some turned to the radical Chinese-led Malayan Communist Party (MCP).

Four months after the creation of the Federation, three European rubber planters were murdered in Perak – the first victims in a guerrilla war launched from jungle enclaves by communist rebels, using the arms caches left by the disbanded Malayan People's Anti-Japanese Army. The British sent in troops, but the killing continued. The violence reached a climax in 1951, with the assassination of High Commissioner Henry Gurney.

Gurney's successor, General Gerald Templer, stepped in to deal with the 'Emergency'. He intensified military action, while cutting the political grass from under the communists' feet. Templer stepped up self-government, increased Chinese access to full citizenship and admitted those of Chinese origin for the first time to the Malayan Civil Service.

Under Cambridge-trained lawyer Tunku Abdul Rahman, brother of the Sultan of Kedah, UMNO's conservative Malays formed an alliance with the English-educated bourgeoisie of the Malayan Chinese and Malayan Indian Congress. Amid the turmoil of the Emergency, Chinese and Indian community leaders wanted a solution. The Alliance won 51 of 52 seats in the 1955 election by promising a fair, multiracial constitution.

Independence

Independence or *merdeka* (freedom) came in 1957, and the Emergency ended three years later. The Alliance's English-educated elite seemed to imagine that multiracial integration would come about through education and employment. With a bicameral government under a constitutional monarchy, the independent Federation made Malay the compulsory national language and Islam the official religion. Primary education could be in Chinese, Indian or English, but secondary education had to be in Malay.

Tunku Abdul Rahman, the first prime minister, reversed his party's anti-Chinese policy by offering Singapore a place in the Federation. With the defeat of Singapore's moderate Progressive Party by left-wing radicals, Tunku Abdul Rahman feared the creation of an independent communist state on his doorstep. As a counterweight to the Singapore Chinese, he brought in the North Borneo states of Sabah and Sarawak, granting them special privileges for their indigenous populations and funds to help develop their backward economies.

To embrace the enlarged territory, the Federation took on the new name of Malaysia in September 1963. But Singapore clashed with Kuala Lumpur over Malay privileges, which Singapore, with its multiracial policies, sought to dismantle. Singapore's effort to reorganise political parties on a social and economic, rather than ethnic, basis misread the temper of the Malay masses. Riots broke out in 1964, and Tunku Abdul Rahman was forced to expel Singapore from the Federation.

In 1967 Penang was hit by serious riots, which showed that political and social harmony could not be taken for granted. Four days of racial riots in the Federal capital in 1969 led to the suspension of the constitution and a state of emergency. The constitution was not restored until February 1971. The riots were a warning for the government, which was passing controversial legislation at the time, such as the granting of special rights to Malays and the restriction of public gatherings.

Tun Abdul Razak, who had played a key role in combating the communist insurrection years earlier, became Prime Minister after the retirement of Tunku Abdul Rahman in 1970. Under his administration, emphasis was placed on improving the status and position of the Malays and 'other indigenous peoples'. The government's aim, over a 20-year period, was to broaden the distribution of wealth held by Malays. The Malay language, *Bahasa Malaysia,* was officially encouraged.

Upon Tun Abdul Razak's death in 1976, Datuk Hussein Onn, a son of the founder of the UMNO, became prime minister, and the UMNO party strengthened its position, at a time when Malaysian exports were also growing. Combined political and economic strength set a sound base for Datuk Seri Dr Mahathir bin Mohamad, when he took up office in July 1981.

The Prime Minister's palatial residence

Under 'the businessmen's prime minister', Dr Mahathir, Malaysia achieved remarkable economic prosperity. Rubber and tin declined as important sources of income but were supplemented by the spread of lucrative palm oil plantations, the discovery of petroleum and natural gas reserves off Borneo's north coast and the peninsula's east coast, and by the development of manufacturing and tourism industries. Timber, which during the 1970s and 1980s brought valuable revenue to Malaysia as a whole and Sabah and Sarawak in particular, was cut back to preserve rainforests. In more recent years, manufacturing, particularly the electronics industry, represented a new direction away from dependence on commodity exports.

The 21st Century

Malaysia entered the new millennium as a wealthy and increasingly economically sound country, aiming to become a fully developed nation by 2020. In October 2003, Datuk Seri Abdullah Ahmad Badawi took over the premiership, following Dr Mathahir's surprise resignation. Abdullah's low-key style has sharply contrasted with that of his combative predecessor. Elections in March 2004 gave the Malaysian prime minister a huge victory, soundly defeating a fundamentalist Muslim party that wanted to impose an Islamic state in Malaysia.

On guard in Kuching

Shielded by Sumatra, Malaysia escaped the worst of the devastation wrought by the Indian Ocean tsunami on 26 December 2004, although around 70 were killed and destruction was caused to coastal villages in Penang, Langkawi, Kedah and Perlis.

Historical Landmarks

c.40,00BC Earliest known habitation at Niah Caves, Sarawak.

c.2,500BC Proto-Malays spread south from Yunnan area in China.

AD500–1000 Development of Hindu-Buddhist trading kingdoms.

1303 Introduction of Islam to the Malay Peninsula.

c.1400 Founding of Melaka by Srivijaya prince Parameswara.

1409 Chinese Admiral Cheng Ho arrives in Melaka.

1411 Parameswara converts to Islam and meets Ming Emperor of China.

1446 Melaka expands under Sultan Muzaffar Shah.

c.1456–98 Prime Minister Tun Perak expands Melaka's empire.

1511 Melaka falls to the Portuguese.

1641 Dutch take Melaka from Portuguese.

1699–1784 Minangkabu-Bugis struggle for domination of Straits of Melaka.

1786 British occupy Penang.

1819 Stamford Raffles negotiates creation of Singapore trading post.

1824 Anglo-Dutch Treaty carves up Malay world into colonial spheres.

1841 James Brooke established as Rajah of Sarawak.

1875–6 Perak War and murder of the British Resident, James Birch.

1896 Federated Malay States (FMS) are created.

1920–41 Early signs of Malay nationalism surface.

1941–5 Japanese conquest and occupation.

1945 British reoccupy Malaysia.

1948 Federation of Malaya inaugurated.

1948–60 Communist uprising – the so-called 'Emergency'.

1955 First general elections in the peninsula; victory for Alliance coalition.

1957 Malaya becomes independent.

1963 Creation of Federation of Malaysia.

1965 Following rioting, Singapore expelled from Federation.

1981–late 2003 Prosperity under Prime Minister Dr Mahathir.

1998 Deputy PM Anwar Ibrahim arrested. KL hosts Commonwealth Games.

2004 Dr Mahathir's successor, Abdullah Ahmed Badawi, wins resoundingly in general elections. Case against Ibrahim overturned. Tidal waves caused by a major earthquake in the Indian Ocean hit Penang and Kedah states.

WHERE TO GO

Setting your priorities in Malaysia before you start out is essential to making your trip both pleasant and satisfying. Happily, many destinations offer a key that active travellers will be searching for, such as exploring Malaysia's culture and history or engaging in a sport like fishing. Often there is an added bonus: a nearby jungle or a beach-side resort.

Malaysia's well developed transport infrastructure – both road and air – also offers the chance to step away from rigid planning if you desire to stay an extra day by the beach or want to do some more extensive shopping. Caution is needed if you are not used to a hot and humid climate and often requires a little extra planning when heading out on tour, trekking or just lazing by the pool.

Planning the Journey

The towns hold a mirror to Malaysia's ethnic blend of Malay, Chinese, Indians and Eurasians, living side by side or in their separate neighbourhoods. The northeast coast of Malaysia, especially between Kota Bharu and Kuantan, is one of the best places to see traditional Malay life with its rich Muslim culture, particularly evident in the *kampungs* (villages) of the interior. Step back into Malaysia's history in the port towns of Melaka or Kota Kinabalu, where colonial rivals once battled for supremacy, and where princes and sultans dealt in palace intrigue. Your attention will also be caught by the beauty of the many mosques, temples, churches and shrines as the country's faithful practise their beliefs. In Melaka, observe the way of life of the Babas, the oldest Chinese community, and its more modern manifestation in Penang.

Sunset on the peninsula's beautiful east coast

Beyond city limits you will find myriad opportunities to enjoy rural and forested Malaysia. But finding your way around the riches of rainforest, coral reef or marine reserve can be bewildering if you plunge in unprepared. Unless you already have some experience in the region, we recommend that you use the services of one of the many first-class local tour operators *(see page 176)*.

Malaysia has done a fine job of giving visitors access to its natural treasures without 'taming' those treasures too much. At the heart of the peninsula, the huge Taman Negara gives you the most comprehensive view of the country's animals and plants in their wild state. A more 'compact' approach is possible on the islands, such as Tioman or Langkawi.

On the island of Borneo, the great natural attractions are Sarawak's caves at Niah and Mulu, river cruises with a visit to tribal longhouses, Sabah's national parks of Mount Kinabalu

Beautiful Emerald Bay Beach on Pangkor Laut Island

and the offshore islands, and the Sepilok wildlife sanctuary. If your main desire is to escape the coastal heat, highland retreats will refresh and invigorate, offering a chance to enjoy what was once the exclusive domain of colonial administrators.

> **Physical displays of affection, such as holding hands or kissing in public, are frowned upon. Do not offer your hand to be shaken unless the other person extends their hand first.**

White sandy beaches and gentle sea breezes are for many the perfect recipe for a holiday from the stresses of modern life, and in Malaysia the offerings are plenty. Whether on the peninsula or at the marine parks of Sabah and Sarawak, you'll find many opportunities to bask and laze under the tropical sun. (Remember to use sunscreen and drink plenty of water to avoid sunburn and dehydration.)

On the west coast the best beaches are at the island resorts of Penang and Langkawi. Unspoiled stretches of fine sand can also be found on the east coast, from Pantai Cahaya Bulan, north of Kota Bharu, down to Beserah, north of Kuantan. Farther south are the resorts of Tioman Island and Desaru. In East Malaysia, Kuching and Kota Kinabalu both have fine hotel resorts.

THE CENTRE

Malaysia's prosperity in recent decades is most evident in the central region of the peninsula, where signs of wealth abound, from the new international airport to KL's dramatic skyline, to members of the middle class driving Malaysian-made Proton sedans on six-lane highways. But even as a new light-rail system wends its way through the capital, progress has not entirely buried the past under chrome and concrete. Still thriving are the old commercial areas that brought so much of the wealth to the city and country generally.

Kuala Lumpur International Airport is one of the biggest in Asia

Beyond KL, the British colonial past – whose structures now more often stand in the shadow of KL's new skyscrapers – continues to echo amid the northern hill stations. Here, amid the cool afternoon breezes or gentle mountain mists of the Cameron Highlands, the English palate for tea (on a plantation scale) and strawberries still thrives. Retreats within easier reach of the city – the casino of the Genting Highlands or theme parks born out of former tin mines – draw Malaysian families for holiday entertainment, a far cry from the more traditional parks, zoos and aquariums.

Commerce and industry line the way to the port city of Klang on the coast, while Ipoh is Perak state's most flourishing tin town, and Kuala Kangsar is the leisurely, royal state capital. The vast Taman Negara, which translates simply as national park, is one of the best preserved primary rainforests in the world, at once accessible to the public and lovingly protective of its plants and wildlife.

Kuala Lumpur

At times **Kuala Lumpur** appears to be a criss-cross of pedestrian-unfriendly overpasses and expressways. But the city opens to islands of almost jungle-like tree-cover before descending again into lively market centres surrounded by the buildings that look down upon the city's busy streets. Visitors may initially be drawn to the 88-storey Petronas Twin Towers or the KL Communications Tower, which are potent symbols of modern Kuala Lumpur. But the more fascinating splendours of the past are closer to street level, where distinctive neo-Gothic styles are beautifully preserved.

As in other Malaysian cities, the population is predominantly Chinese. The Chinese community is prominent in the modern business world. Chinatown itself remains a hive of bustling activity, standing cheek by jowl with a Little India of pungent spice shops and ornate Hindu temples. Ethnic Malays are present in the upper echelons of the government, civil service and tourist offices.

The Historic Centre

KL's main historic quarter lies near Jalan Sultan Hishamuddin, where, on the east side of the broad avenue, is the **Sultan Abdul Samad Building**. The handsome crypto-Moorish Federal Secretariat, now the **Supreme Court** and **High Court**, was begun in 1894 (finished in 1897) and capped

KL's modern skyline with the Royal Selangor Club in the foreground

Sultan Abdul Samad Building

with three copper onion-shaped domes. One tops a 40-m (120-ft) high clock tower that suggests inspiration from Big Ben in London. That is perhaps not a surprise, since the building was designed by British architect A.C. Norman.

Among the many impressive skyscrapers, one of the most striking is the 35-storey **Dayabumi Complex** (1970), southeast of Dataran Merdeka. The soaring white tower successfully integrates traditional Islamic architectural themes – pointed arches, delicate open tracery – with otherwise modern design. Included in the southernmost end of the complex is the adjoining **Pejabat Pos Besar** (General Post Office), built in a similar modern Islamic style, and a shopping mall.

On the western side of the boulevard is the **Dataran Merdeka** (Freedom Square). In colonial days, the sound of a cricket bat would have been heard as the rays of the afternoon sun stretched across the field. It was here that members of the mock-Tudor **Royal Selangor Club** (1884), also designed by A.C. Norman, took time off from the affairs of the Empire to play cricket. On the wide lawn independence was greeted by cheers on 31 August 1957. The Anglican **St Mary's Cathedral** is found on the square's northern side. The oldest church in KL, it began life in 1887 as a wooden shack on Bukit Aman before being relocated here. The present building was designed by A.C. Norman and remains a centre of worship and spiritual life for Anglicans in the city.

A.C. Norman was rivalled in commissions by A.B. Hubbock, whose work is reflected in the **Malaysian Railway** buildings and headquarters, located south on Jalan Sultan Hishamuddin. The main station (completed in 1911 and extensively renovated in 1986) resembles a gleaming sultan's palace and is more attractive than the sombre brown headquarters building across the street. A fine example of Moorish architecture, it reflects the Ottoman and Mogul glory of the 13th and 14th centuries. The north wing was bombed in World War II, and the second floor was gutted by fire in 1968.

Hubbock also designed the **Masjid Jamek**. Since 1909 this building has marked the confluence of the Gombak and Klang Rivers, where tin miners loaded supplies to be sent upriver and unloaded their tin for shipment west to Port Klang, and where the city's roots were set down. It was designed in 1907 by Hubbock in an Indian Moghul style: three-pointed domes over the prayer hall, two minarets and balustrades above an arcade of cusped arches – the whole predominantly gleaming white, with pink terracotta brick.

KL Railway Station at night

Across the river going east from the Dayabumi Complex is the old **Pasar Seni** (Central Market), set in an attractive art deco building (1936) in pastel blue and pink with a bold,

A multicultural city

bright skylit roof over a buff-tiled floor. Clothes and Malaysian arts and crafts have replaced the fish, meat and vegetables that used to be sold here, but the fine old marble counters have not been touched.

Chinatown

Southeast from the Central Market lie the exotic offerings of **Chinatown**, within the boundaries of Jalan Sultan, Jalan Bandar (now known as Jalan Tun H.S. Lee), and especially along **Jalan Petaling**. You will find everything from Chinese apothecaries who display their medicines in porcelain jars, to Nepalese traders offering exotic jewellery, from fortune-tellers to pet shops.

At night, when Jalan Petaling is closed to traffic, the area comes alive. Pedlars sell replica watches, music, videos, clothing, jewellery and ornaments; the side streets are full of open-air restaurants offering barbecued meat, seafood, noodles, rice-pots and do-it-yourself 'steamboats' *(see page 162)*.

Past the Jalan Tun H.S. Lee and Jalan Cheng Lock junction is the **Sze Ya Temple**, founded by Yap Ay Loy, a city leader in KL's early days. The largest temple is **Chan See Shu Yuen**, built in 1906 and dedicated to Chong Wah, a Sung dynasty emperor. It also marks Chinatown's southern boundary.

One of the breathtaking displays of colour comes soon after the Kwoong Siew Association Temple, in the **Sri Mahamari-amman Hindu Temple** on Jalan Bandar, on the west side of Chinatown. It was built in the style of a south Indian *gopuram* (temple gatehouse-tower), covered with a riot of colourful statuary from the Hindu pantheon. First erected in 1873, it was shunted across to its present site to make way for the railway station in 1855, and it is from here the annual Thaipusam pilgrimage to the Batu Caves *(see page 51)* commences.

North and east of the historic centre is KL's 'Golden Triangle', a newer office, entertainment and shopping district. Nearby are two of the city's tallest landmarks. The **Petronas Twin Towers** are located north of the triangle and known officially as the **Kuala Lumpur City Centre (KLCC)**. On the 41st and 42nd floors there is a sky bridge open to the public, and below there is a concert hall and upmarket shopping mall. For the best views of the city and beyond try the **Menara Kuala Lumpur** (Communications Tower) which opened in 1996 and rises to 421m (1,381ft) on the western edge

Shopping in the KLCC

of the district. The non-stop lift takes 55 seconds from ground to the observatory, and offers spectacular views. For those wanting to eat on the move, there is the Seri Angkasa revolving restaurant on the level above.

Cultural and Historical Sights

To the west of the railway station and within view is the **Masjid Negara** (National Mosque), a modern complex covering over 5 hectares (13 acres). On Friday and other important religious days it can house 8,000 worshippers under the tent-like stone roof of its Grand Hall. Walls of open-work stone tracery support a canopy of 18 folds fanning out in a circle. These symbolise the 13 states of Malaysia and 5 pillars of Islamic faith. The mosque includes ceremonial rooms, a library, a meeting hall and a mausoleum for national heroes, set around cool pools mirroring the blue stained glass of the Grand Hall and marble galleries. Soaring above it all is a 73-m (239-ft) high minaret, with a balcony from which the *muezzin* calls the faithful to prayer.

The **Muzium Negara** (National Museum) stands on Jalan Damansara south of the Lake Gardens. The building, opened in 1963, blends modern and traditional Malay design. Two glass mosaic murals flanking the entrance depict cultural and historical themes. There are five main galleries dedicated to such subjects as history, national sports and natural history.

Other museums include the nearby **Islamic Arts Museum Malaysia**, which showcases the art and culture of the Islamic

The National Mosque among the skyscrapers of downtown KL

world. The **National History Museum** on Jalan Raja south of the Dataran Merdeka, with exhibits dating back 520 million years (metamorphic sandstone), as well as a 40,000-year-old *homo sapiens* skull.

> *Lebuh* is Malay for street, *Jalan* means road and *Bukit* means hill.

The older **Royal Malaysian Police Museum** (1961) on Jalan Semarak highlights the war against the communist insurgents from 1948 to 1960, known as the Emergency *(see page 30)*. On the campus of the University of Malaysia is the **Asian Art Museum**, with exhibits of sculptures and textiles from within the region. Given the extent of wealth it has brought to the country, it is not surprising to have a **Natural Rubber Museum**, which opened in 1992 at the Rubber Research Institute's Experimental Station in Sungai Buloh.

Taman Tasik Perdana (The Lake Gardens)

West of the Masjid Negara are the **Taman Tasik Perdana** (Lake Gardens), 91 hectares (225 acres) of parkland landscaped in 1888 under British Resident Frank Swettenham, for the citizens' relaxation. A popular place for picnicking, jogging and resting beneath the trees, it features a boating lake and provides a lovely escape from the city's tensions. There is also a butterfly farm, orchid garden, deer park and bird park, the latter home to more than 5,000 birds. Within the bounds of the gardens is a **Planetarium** and a space theme park.

Set on a hill at the northern end of the park across a main road, the **Tugu Kebangsaan** (National Monument) commemorates Malaysia's recent dark history through the years of the Emergency. The bronze group sculpture stands among reflecting pools and fountains with a mosque at one end. Designed by Felix de Weldon, it depicts triumphant flagbearers flanked by armed guards, while another soldier helps a wounded comrade. Beneath them sprawl the enemy's dead. Also on the National Monument grounds is a **Cenotaph** to the British Commonwealth's dead of the two World Wars. West of the monument, just outside the park, is the 18-storey **Parliament House**, which holds the sessions of the Senate and House of Representatives.

Away From the City Centre

To see the **tin magnates' mansions** that remain standing, take a taxi ride on Jalan Ampang some 10km (6 miles) north-west of town. A few of these grand 19th- and 20th-century residences survive, tucked away among the skyscrapers, the jungle often invading the gardens. They offer insight into the wealth amassed by the tin magnates during their heyday.

One of the best preserved is the Dewan Tunku Abdul Rahman, built in 1935 by Chinese tin and rubber mogul Eu Tong Sen. Nowadays it is the **Malaysia Tourism Centre**, which provides travel advice, brochures, computer workstations and banking services. The complex includes a shopping arcade, police station and facilities for cultural shows.

A taxi or train to the **National Stadium** at Bukit Jalil takes you to the centrepiece of Malaysia's site for the 1998 Commonwealth Games. The spectacular stadium has a capacity of 100,000; nearby there is a 4,000-seat Aquatic Centre, as well as two hockey stadiums, a squash centre, an indoor stadium and an outdoor family park.

Malaysia Tourism Centre

While the number of major department stalls and malls ever increases, night markets remain a favourite throughout Malaysia for good deals and excellent local food. They are ideal for soaking up local colour and atmosphere. The cheapest of the markets is at **Chow Kit**, where Batu Road crosses Jalang Dang Wangi. Another market catering to more traditional tastes is the **Kampung Bahru** (New Village), behind the Chow Kit area. This market is a *Pasar Minggu* (Sunday Market), but like so many other similar markets throughout the country, it begins late on Saturday afternoon and trades on into the early hours of Sunday morning.

The Blue Mosque in Shah Alam, the capital of Selangor

Day Trips from Kuala Lumpur

Around Kuala Lumpur is the state of **Selangor**, an area that grew rich on tin and today is Malaysia's wealthiest and most developed state. While the emphasis in this region is clearly on industry, information technology and administration, there are a number of sites well worth a visit.

Shah Alam

Constructed in the 1970s out of rubber plantations, **Shah Alam** is the capital of Selangor and is one of the country's best-planned cities with large houses and broad, tree-lined boulevards. The city's standout landmark is the state mosque, the **Masjid Sultan Salahuddin Abdul Aziz Shah**, also known as ◀

the Blue Mosque because of its distinctive blue dome, which is bigger than that of St Paul's Cathedral in London. The mosque is laid out in the style of the Great Mosque of Mecca, with a worship hall that can accommodate 16,000 worshippers. When touring the interior of the mosque, ensure that you are appropriately dressed (remember to remove your footwear), and that it is not prayer time. Within the grounds there are landscaped gardens and a pool that links up to the Shah Alam lake gardens.

Theme Parks

As prosperity has taken hold in Malaysia, so too has the style of entertainment. Just beyond the city there are several theme parks built out of the remains of the gorges created from tin mining. The **Mines Wonderland** has been built on what was the world's largest open-cast mining operation. South of Kuala Lumpur along Jalan Sungai Besi, it includes snow-making facilities for a winter feel in the tropics. **Sunway**

Thaipusam Festival in the Batu Caves

The Batu Caves are the focus of the great Thaipusam Festival celebrating Lord Murugan receiving a sacred spear with which to vanquish the sources of evil.

Every January or February thousands of Hindus gather to do penitence for past sins. The most fervent of them punish themselves by having their tongues or cheeks pierced with skewers, and hooks inserted in their bodies. Some also carry a *kavadi* (a frame bearing peacock feathers and statuettes of deities). Some simply carry jars of milk, rose-water, coconut or sugar-cane juice. During Thaipusam, as many as 500,000 people will crowd around the Batu Caves.

For infidel tourists, the climb in humid heat up 272 steps to the cave-shrine entrance may be penitence enough. Beneath the caves lie dozens of underground limestone vaults.

Lagoon in Bandar Sunway, located near Selangor's capital, Shah Alam, is known for its water attractions and rides and is great for entertaining the children.

Batu Caves

The giant **Batu Caves** are a popular excursion 45 minutes' drive north of town just off the Ipoh Road. Set in limestone cliffs hidden in the jungle, they were 'discovered' in 1878 by a group of explorers, among them the American naturalist William Hornaday. The caves were a hideout for anti-Japanese, communist guerrillas during World War II. Now transformed into a Hindu shrine, they receive the most attention during the Thaipusam festival celebrated in the early months of each year.

The Batu Caves, once a military hideout, now a Hindu shrine

There are in fact dozens of impressive underground limestone vaults attracting botanists and zoologists to witness their unique flora and fauna, but only three caves are open to the general public. At the top of a 272-step staircase is the **Cathedral Cave**, the most breathtaking of the three, with its architectural columns of lofty stalactites and stalagmites. At the foot of the hill, a bridge over a pond leads to the **Art Gallery Cave**, with displays of garish statues of Hindu deities, and the **Poet's Cave**, where verses of the ancient Tamil poet Thiruvalluvar are painted directly on stone tablets. These two-line *kural* verses deal variously with such fundamental issues as morals, wisdom, love and finances.

Templer Park

Farther north (another 9 km/6 miles along the Ipoh Road) from the Batu Caves is **Templer Park**, which offers the sights of a Malaysian rainforest to those with little time to venture into the major national parks and forested areas. Britain's last High Commissioner, Sir Gerald Templer, conceived the park as a 'vast jungle retreat for the public' in 1950. Covering an area of 1,200 hectares (2,965 acres), the rainforest comes complete with waterfalls, rushing streams, lagoons for swimming and caves in the Bukit Takun limestone cliffs to explore. There are several clearly defined paths, with the highest point being **Bukit Takun** 740m (2,428ft) on the western side of the river in the park's northern corner.

Breezy hill stations offer refuge from the tropical heat

The Highlands

By the time Malaysia came under the British imperial sway in the late 18th century, colonial officials had fully developed the grand institution of the hill station, where they could cool off from the hot and humid lowlands in the days before air-conditioning. These havens of relaxation have now become holiday resorts, set among golf courses, gardens and orchards in the mountain ranges of the peninsula's interior. Nowadays, Malaysian families are lured to the highlands closest to Kuala Lumpur – Genting and Fraser's Hill – while the Cameron Highlands is the most popular region for foreign visitors. These retreats offer everything from casinos to horse riding, golf to jungle trekking, depending on the location.

> **The jungles, especially in the Cameron Highlands, were once the strongholds for rebels during the Emergency, so some caution is required when venturing into undeveloped areas; good maps are a must, and on occasion a guide would be recommended.**

Genting Highlands

Nearest of the highland resort areas to Kuala Lumpur at 51km (32 miles), the **Gentings** rise to 2,000m (6,560ft) and are a far cry from the peaceful, misty, forested mountains they were just two decades ago. Nowadays, descriptions of the resort and hotel complex vary from simply noisy to a 'one-stop destination for fantasy, excitement and adventure'. You'll find a wide range of facilities here, from an 18-hole golf course to a theme park with cinemas, a monorail, boat-rides and restaurants – even a 32-lane, ten-pin bowling centre. The resort's casino is Malaysia's only such legal gambling house, with strict dress codes requiring men to wear ties or long-sleeved batik shirts.

Fraser's Hill

In contrast to the Genting Highlands, this charming, old-fashioned hill station, located 100km (60 miles) northwest of KL, is built across seven hills, its highest point being 1,500m (4,920ft) in the Titiwangsa mountain range. These days it offers a retreat for Malaysia's business set. The resort was named after Louis James Fraser, an English adventurer and scoundrel, who dealt in mule hides, tin, opium and gambling. Fraser had disappeared mysteriously before the hill station came into being, in 1910.

Road access may be difficult, with the last 8km (5 miles) along a winding, narrow roadway where an alternating, one-way traffic system is in place. It was along this portion of road, marked by a signpost that reads 'Emergency Historical Site', where British High Commissioner Sir Henry Gurney was killed during the height of the communist insurgency in 1951.

The countryside is wilder and less cultivated than that in the Cameron Highlands, but the sedate side of colonial life is also more recognisable here in the white-and-grey stone bungalows with roses, rhododendrons, poinsettias, holly-

---

Alfred Russel Wallace, Nature Sleuth

A contemporary of Charles Darwin, Alfred Russel Wallace proved a true detective in his pioneering research in evolution theory and 'bio-geography' – the geographical distribution of animals. In Malaysia, he is best known as the 'discoverer' of the national butterfly, the green-and-black 'Rajah Brooke Birdwing'. But his most intriguing contributions came in the field of natural mimicry. Beyond the familiar camouflage techniques of chameleons and stick-insects, he watched viceroy butterflies trick birds by cultivating a resemblance to the monarch butterfly, which the birds hate. He also discovered ant-eating spiders that look like their prey.

hocks and dahlias in the gardens. You'll find a range of accommodation on offer, from Fraser's Pine and Silverpark Resorts in the top tier to more middle-range inns, bungalows and even a youth hostel. There are good tennis courts, a nine-hole golf course, playgrounds and even opportunities for horse riding.

Many rare butterfly species are found in the Cameron Highlands

Several nature trails are also marked out through the nearby forests, and the wealth of wildlife means that jungle rambles are particularly enjoyable. Swimming is possible at the **Jeriau Waterfall**, some 4½km (2 miles) north of town. Birdwatchers should look out for more than 270 species of birds, which may be seen in the immediate area. Each June, the Malaysian Nature Society supports an 'international bird race', where teams compete to identify the largest number of birds.

Cameron Highlands

The finest of the cool hill resorts, 240km (150 miles) from KL, stands on a splendid plateau in rolling green valleys, surrounded by the rugged granite peaks of the Titiwangsa Range, the tallest of which is Mount Brinchang at 2,032m (6,664ft). If you've been travelling on the coast, or elsewhere in semi-tropical Southeast Asia, the **Cameron Highlands**, located over 1,520m (4,987ft) above sea level, offer great relief amid morning mists and cool breezes.

Spread over three districts are the townships of **Ringlet**, Tanah Rata (the main township) and **Brinchang**. Ringlet

Extensive tea plantation in the Cameron Highlands

township, the first point of arrival, offers very little that is special, apart from flower nurseries and access to some tea plantations. Continue 13 km (7 miles) from Ringlet to reach Tanah Rata. On the road from Ringlet is the **Sultan Abu Bakar Lake**, an artificial lake that was formed by the damming of the Bertam River. Brinchang, just a few more kilometres beyond Tanah Rata, is known for its farms, flower nurseries, fruit gardens and long-established tea plantations.

The hill station itself was named after William Cameron, a British surveyor, who in 1885 reported the finding of the 'fine plateau'. His 'discovery' was soon followed by tea planters and Chinese vegetable growers. The Highlands also still hold the answer to the mysterious disappearance of wealthy American Thai-silk entrepreneur Jim Thompson, who disappeared one evening in 1967 after going off for a stroll while on holiday at the hill station.

The Highlands are best reached by train on the KL–Butterworth line to Tapah Road station and then by taxi up into the hills. Driving yourself on the narrow winding road with frequent back-ups imposed by trucks in a hurry could be a hazardous business. Let the taxi driver worry about that, while you admire the magnificent scenery changing from lowland mangrove, bamboo and palms, to denser rainforest of lush greenery and, as the heat drops away and the more comfortable mountain air takes over, montane oaks and laurels familiar to temperate climates.

Tanah Rata is festooned with hotels, some good Chinese and Indian restaurants, and a variety of English-style tearooms serving the local Cameronian brew together with cakes and locally grown strawberries with cream. Stores offer everything from the practical to glass-mounted scorpions and butterflies.

A visit to a tea plantation is easily arranged, with a bus service readily available to and from the farms. The main plantations are the **Boh Tea Estate** and the **Sungai Palas** and **Blue Valley** tea estates. Accommodation options in Tanah Rata vary depending on your budget, from the upper tier, offering international-class resorts, such as Strawberry Park, to the moderately priced Cameronian Holiday Inn. Worth a visit – even if you can't afford the room rates – is **Ye Olde Smokehouse** near the golf course. The ivy-covered, mock-Tudor resort has become something of an institution since it was built in the 1930s. An afternoon traditional 'cream tea'

Enjoy a roast dinner or a cream tea at Ye Olde Smokehouse

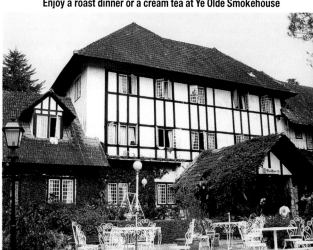

> The tapir is remarkable for two features: its short, overlapping snout that resembles the sawed-off trunk of an elephant, and its unique body colouring – black at the front, white in the middle and back, with black rear legs. With luck you may spot one in Tanah Rata.

or English roast lunch or dinner is an experience in itself. Nearby is a fine 18-hole public golf course, beautifully kept despite the strange hazard of a narrow, concrete-sided canal running through the middle.

The cooler climate makes jungle walks here a special pleasure, not least of all for the myriad brightly coloured butterflies around the waterfalls, with almost a dozen officially listed. Several of the walks pass through – or close to – the Malaysian Agriculture Research Development Institute, just a few kilometres from Tanah Rata.

Two well-marked paths from Tanah Rata, which are easy enough for the whole family, lead to swimming and picnic spots at **Parit Falls** and **Robinson Falls**. Other more challenging choices, for which you should enlist the help of a guide, take you up to **Mount Jasar** (1,696m/5,564ft) and **Mount Berembam** (1,841m/6,040ft). Besides the butterflies, look out for red-bellied squirrels, wild pigs and, if you are lucky, an occasional tapir. The best buys here are fresh flowers, fruit and vegetables.

Perak

A journey to Perak takes the traveller into what once was the key region for Malaysia's economic prosperity, standing as a lure to powerful states and interests as well as (mostly Chinese) migrant workers. Tin, the basis for the state's wealth, was once taken from diggings that claimed to be the largest such mines in the world. The wealth from the mines paid for many of the historical structures evident throughout the state.

Perak, which means silver in Malay, is Malaysia's second largest state, reaching from Tanjung Malim in the south to the Thai border, covering some 21,000 sq km (8,108 sq miles). Its sultan's family is also the last to be able to trace its ancestry to the 16th-century sultans of Melaka.

The capital Ipoh may be considered the capital of the world's tin industry. It superseded Perak's other rich mining capital, Taiping (formerly known as Larut), in this role in 1937. Kuala Kangsar is the royal capital and has been home to Perak's sultans since the 15th century.

The journey north from KL either by train or car takes you through a captivating landscape of jungle, reaching back from the coastal plains to climb the blue hills of the Barisan Titiwangsa Range. Amid this wild beauty, enhanced by spectacular outcrops of limestone rock, are the tell-tale scars of the tin mines of the Kinta Valley.

Ipoh

Once the harbour for all incoming junks and sampans from the Straits of Melaka (Selat Melaka) through the Perak River, the city of **Ipoh** is located on the Kinta River 220km (135 miles) north of KL. Ipoh offers good accommodation and amenities, including a range of restaurants with Chinese specialities, such as steamed chicken with bean sprouts and noodles.

The echoes of colonialism are clearly evident in the **Railway Station**, whose Moorish architecture is reminiscent of KL's central station

Warriors at Perak Museum in Taiping *(see page 63)*

A Buddhist cave temple in Ipoh

and is locally nicknamed 'the Taj Mahal'; nearby is the Majestic Station Hotel. The **High Court** and **Hong Kong and Shanghai Bank** buildings are also excellent examples of architecture from the Edwardian era. Other memories of the British presence are in the **clock tower**, commemorating the first British resident of Perak, James Birch, who was assassinated in 1875. **St Michael's School** and the **Royal Ipoh Club** are also monuments of the former colonial era.

Around Jalan Dato' Sagor and the nearby streets are some of the best preserved examples of **Chinese architecture** in Malaysia. For insight into the local tin mining industry, visit the excellent **Geological Museum** on Jalan Sultan Azlan Shah. In addition to exhibits of Perak's rich variety of minerals, ores and fossils are models of tin mining equipment. The **Darul Ridzuan Museum**, housed in the former home of Malay dignitaries, chronicles the history and development of Ipoh.

Outside the city, amid vast caves in limestone outcrops, are a number of Buddhist temples. In the south the **Sam Poh Tong** temples are nestled within high limestone caves and cavities near **Gunung Rapat**. The latter dates back to 1890s, while the present façade was built in the 1950s, with the temple still home to a group of monks and nuns. Six kilometres (4 miles) north of Ipoh is the **Perak Tong**, built in 1926 by a Buddhist priest from China. Here the main attraction is a 13-m (41-ft) sitting Buddha within the eerie darkened cavern; altogether there are more than 40 Buddha statues.

Saved from the over-growth of foliage in the past two decades, 12km (7 miles) from Ipoh is **Kellie's Castle**, a mansion whose construction was halted when its owner, William Kellie Smith, a rubber planter, died in Portugal in the mid-1920s. Further south, in **Teluk Intan**, is Malaysia's equivalent of the leaning tower of Pisa. The pagoda-like structure, built in 1885, is 25.5m (84ft) tall and was once used for water storage.

Kuala Kangsar

Home to the sultans of Perak for the past 500 years, **Kuala Kangsar** is built on a sweep of the Perak River (Sungei Perak) 50km (32 miles) from Ipoh on a newer highway. The town has two royal palaces; the brash stone residence **Istana Iskandariah**, and the more elegant traditional timbered **Istana Kenangan**, now used as a Royal Museum.

Kellie's Castle was destined never to be finished

The striking domes and minarets of the Ubadiah Mosque, one of the most photographed Muslim buildings in Malaysia

This is also where Malaysia's rubber industry started, with the planting of nine seedlings by former resident Hugh Low in 1877. One of the originals still survives near the district office on Jalan Raja Bendahara. The most striking building, set on a grass mound, is the **Ubadiah Mosque**, with its massive golden dome of glowing copper set in a nest of white. Begun in 1917, its construction was interrupted on several occasions, most dramatically when two elephants of the Sultan Idris went on a rampage on the imported Italian marble floor.

Kuala Kangsar has long been famous for **Malay College**, set amid spacious grounds near the centre of town. This has been a prestigious and exclusive school for the education of the children of the Malay aristocracy since it was founded by the British in 1904. It is now open to the best (Malay) scholars of all classes.

Taiping

Another 30 minutes' drive from Kuala Kangsar, the old mining town of **Taiping** was formerly known as Larut. Its present-day name, meaning 'everlasting peace', was proposed by Britain as part of its diplomatic contribution to the end of the bloody feuds between Chinese secret societies fighting over control of the tin mining industry in the 1870s. They were forced to end their conflict under the Treaty of Pangkor in 1874, after British intervention.

Happily boasting the peninsula's heaviest rainfalls, Taiping, the former capital of Perak state, is now a sleepy town full of large trees overhanging the wide streets. It has a magnificent 62-hectare (153-acre) park, **Lake Gardens**, landscaped from a tin mine abandoned in 1890, then owned by Chung Keng Kwee. The grounds are now home to a 9-hole golf course, a small zoo, which offers a night safari tour, and an old **Government Rest House** (now a hotel).

Built in 1883, the **Perak Museum**, housing an interesting display of ancient weapons and Orang Asli implements, is the oldest in Malaysia. On the way, you will pass the **prison**, used by the Japanese in World War II and then for guerrilla troops captured during the Emergency. Built in 1885, the prison today is where most of the executions of Malaysia's drug offenders are carried out.

Beyond the Lake Gardens, the **Taiping War Cemetery** bears impressive witness to the peninsula's early role in the Pacific War against the Japanese. The tombs of men of the Royal Australian Air Force, Indian Army Corps of Clerks, Ambulance Sepoy of the Indian Army Medical Corps and Royal Air Force reveal that many of them died on the very first day of active duty: 8 December 1941.

Once a tea estate, cool, cloud-enshrouded **Bukit Larut** (Maxwell Hill), 12km (7½ miles) northeast of Taiping, was Malaysia's smallest and oldest hill station and the retreat for colonial administrators. At 1,035m (3,400ft) above sea level, it has great views when the misty rain-clouds break. Near the jeep terminal, pretty bungalows and rest houses offer rooms for rent, with balconies overlooking the valley, but you must book in advance. The walk to the summit is signposted, and upon reaching the top on a clear day it is possible to view the sweep of coastline from Penang to Pangkor.

Pulau Pangkor

The largest of the nine islands lying offshore in the Straits of Melaka is **Pulau Pangkor**. Its beaches offer aquatic activities and there are nearby jungle walks. The ferry from Lumut,

Night falls on Pangkor Laut

about 50km (31 miles) south of Taiping, to Pangkor Island takes about 45 minutes. Once there, you'll find the wide sands of the **Pantai Puteri Dewi** (Beach of the Beautiful Princess) along the 122-hectare (301-acre) island's northern shore. A private retreat and one of the most exclusive destinations in Asia, **Pangkor Laut Resort** tends to attract the well-heeled tourist.

Taman Negara

The grand **Taman Negara** national park provides an ideal setting for exploring the vast expanses of rainforest, fast-flowing rivers and mountains of the peninsula's

Main Range. It covers a huge area of 4,343 sq km (1,676 sq miles), spreading across three states: Pahang, Terengganu and Kelantan.

Backpackers may want to go it alone, but most people are advised to plan their visit

> **Before visiting Taman Negara, be sure to buy your film, batteries, bottled water, insect-repellent, etc. Every-thing is more expensive inside the park.**

through a tour operator in KL or before they leave for Malaysia. Armed with an entry permit, visitors make first for the park headquarters, 300km (187 miles) northeast of the national capital by road via Jerantut and 60km (37 miles) by motor-powered longboat from Kuala Tembeling.

The **boat ride** on the Tembeling River is likely to be one of the highlights of your visit. Along the way, you will see aboriginal Negrito fishermen – the only human residents allowed by park authorities to stay here – setting or check-ing their nets. Keep a look out, too, for water buffalo taking a soak, river lizards slipping in and out of the water and looking as large as crocodiles (the latter do not come this far upstream), and even an occasional otter. Among the birds, you will see the flash of a kingfisher or hornbill. Wear a hat and bring along plenty of bottled water. The journey usually takes about three hours, even longer when short stretches of the river dry up, forcing passengers to walk along the riverbank while the boatmen push the launch through the shallows.

The headquarters at **Kuala Tahan** have a good range of accommodation – chalets, a hostel and a rest house – plus washing facilities, restaurants and a grocery store. Payment is strictly in Malaysian currency. *(For your trekking require-ments, see page 176.)* The park headquarters organise infor-mative evening slide-shows as a general introduction to the features of the surrounding rainforest.

River rapids make for a wild ride

Jungle Trails

There are marked trails leading from the park's headquarters into the jungle. Guides use them for organised walking and boat tours, but you can, of course, go off with your own group. There are both day trips and overnight tours to observation-hides, from where you can watch for wildlife visiting nearby salt-licks and watering holes. Overnight stays are organised at several observation-hides in the region, namely at **Kumbang**, **Yong**, **Tabing**, **Belau** and **Cegar Anjing**. Park headquarters will provide sheets if you do not have a sleeping bag. You should be in the hide by the afternoon and out again the next morning at around 9.30am. From park headquarters, day trips leaving in the early morning include a walk to Bukit Indah, followed by a boat ride through the rapids to **Kuala Trenggan**, returning to headquarters on foot; a walk to the **Tabing Hide**, followed by a boat ride to the **Lata Berkoh** rapids, then another trek back to headquarters; a boat ride on the Tembeling River to the **Gua Telinga Bat Cave**, which you enter on hands and knees until you can stand. You then find yourself in a great vault inhabited by hundreds of fruit- and insect-eating bats (not at all interested in attacking humans). Only the squeamish will object to the giant toads and harmless little white cave-racer snakes.

The most adventurous trek for experienced climbers is a full nine-day walk up and down the peninsula's highest peak, **Mount Tahan** (2,187m/7,173ft) high. A jungle guide accompanies the group.

Flora and Fauna

The dipterocarp rainforest here includes the *tualang* tree. At 50m (164ft), it is the tallest tree in Southeast Asia. Among the exotic jungle fruit are mango, durian, rambutan and wild banana. At heights above 1,500m (5,000ft), you will see montane oaks and conifers.

With patience and luck by day, or rotating shift watches by night, you may see wild pigs, sambars, barking deer, gibbons, pig-tailed macaques, leaf monkeys, tree shrews or red flying squirrels. Visitors to the Kumbang Hide have sometimes caught sight of rare tigers and leopards.

During the fruit season, birdwatchers have spotted up to 70 species just around the park headquarters. Among them are lesser fish eagles, crested serpent eagles, osprey, peacock pheasants and garnet pitta. From September to March you can also see migrant Arctic warblers, Japanese paradise flycatchers and Siberian blue robins.

Even if you do not spot much of the wildlife mentioned here – and you are bound to see something – the sheer experience of the jungle at night, with its incredible noises, the flitting of mysterious fireflies and the sense of invisible but omnipresent life and movement around you will make it all worthwhile.

Taman Negara's frog life

THE WEST COAST

For the romantics, the township names of Port Dickson and
Melaka (formerly Malacca) on the West Coast evoke stories
of the glorious past of sailing ships and Chinese junks carrying spices, silks and gold, of pirates and cutlasses, of noble
men and beautiful princesses. In many ways, this is the story
of southwestern Malaysia's southwest coastline. Nowadays,
the rich tapestry of history lies in the monuments and homes
as well as the descendants of the colonisers – Malay and Indian, Chinese, Portuguese, Dutch and British. In the far north,
Penang is both a holiday destination and a commercial centre,
while closer to the border with Thailand, Pulau Langkawi is a
top resort destination for those in search of white sands, gentle
seas, scenic landscape and duty-free goods.

**Melaka, Malaysia's first major city, is a patchwork quilt of architectural
styles and international influences**

South from Kuala Lumpur to Melaka

The highway from Kuala Lumpur and Selangor leads through Negeri Sembilan, the 'nine states' federated as one in the 18th century. You travel past the vast palm oil and rubber plantations to the state capital of Seremban, 64km (40 miles) southwest of Kuala Lumpur.

Seremban

Here, the distinctive Min-angkabau buffalo-horn roofs of Sumatran heritage are evident, together with the

> **Negeri Sembilan's ruler is not a sultan but a Yam Tuan Besar or Yang Di Pertuan Besar, meaning 'He Who is Greatest'.**

more recent colonial Victorian style and the traditions of Chinese commercial shophouses. The main attractions are the **State Legislative Assembly Building**, a nest of nine roofs, one for each founding state; and the **Taman Seni Budaya Negeri** (Arts and Culture Complex). Visit the state museum located within the complex, where weapons as well as brass and silverware and a tableau portraying a grand royal wedding are on display. In the grounds opposite is the **Kampung Ampang Tinggi**, a Malay prince's residence built entirely of wood. The neoclassical **State Library**, with its imposing colonial façade, was once the State Secretarial Building. Situated opposite are the extensive Lake Gardens.

Sri Menanti

For what is probably the best original example of Minang-kabau architecture, take a side trip to the old royal capital, 37km (23 miles) east of Seremban on the Kuala Pilah Road. The ruler's palace, **Istana Lama**, was the official residence of the royal family until 1931, replacing an earlier palace which had burnt down. The palace features 99 pillars, denoting 99 warriors of various *luak* (clans).

Melaka

Easily reached by taxi or express bus from KL, **Melaka** (Malacca) was Malaysia's first city. It was built on the trading empires of spices and textiles and a history soaked in the blood of battles as rival colonial powers challenged each other to take hold of the port. In its glorious 15th-century heyday, it was the most vital port in Southeast Asia, with as many as 2,000 ships docked here. The city's sultans expanded their territorial reach, using from the wealth gained from trade, extending as far as Pahang and Singapore and even to the east coast of Sumatra. Today, even as the highrise makes its presence felt, the colonial past remains in the architecture and monuments. The city's Chinatown, especially along Jalan Hang Jebat, is a haven for antiques buyers.

The Old Centre

The main buildings of historical or cultural significance are all within easy walking distance of the old centre, Dutch Square, down by the Melaka River.

The square is situated just off **Melaka Bridge**. Spanning the river, the bridge was once the town's main strategic link between port and city and the site of major battles against the European invaders.

The most prominent building overlooking the square is the Dutch **Stadthuys** (Town Hall), dating from around 1650. It was originally the official residence of Dutch governors and their officers. Behind the red façade is a structure built of masonry hauled from the Portuguese citadel. Since 1980 the building has housed the Museum of Ethnography and History, tracing the town's colonial and Malay past.

The **Jam Besar** (Clock Tower) was built in 1886 by the family of a Chinese merchant, Tan Koon Chang. In the middle of the square is the **Queen Victoria Jubilee Fountain**, flanked by a mouse-deer, recalling the legendary little beast that inspired Prince Parameswara to make Melaka his capital *(see panel on page 18)*.

Christ Church, with an imposing red exterior, was built between 1741 and 1753, in commemoration of the centenary of the Dutch occupation. Additions to the church were made by the British in the 19th century. Each of the long ceiling beams of the interior is hewn from one tree. Equally impressive are the massive, hand-made wooden pews, an original feature.

The archway and gate of the **A Famosa** fortress is all that remains of the 16th-century Portuguese fort next to the Stadthuys. It was saved from total destruction by Sir Stamford Raffles, then a government secretary in Penang. The date, 1670, and coat of arms were added to the gateway by the Dutch East India Company. The gate steps lead to the remains of **St Paul's Church**, built by a Portuguese captain, Duarte Coelho, as a chapel in 1521. Originally known as the Church of Our Lady of the Annunciation, it was renamed by the Dutch, who captured Melaka in 1641, and fell into disuse when Christ Church was built. In front of the church tower is a **statue of St Francis Xavier**, the Spanish Jesuit missionary who visited Melaka several times from 1545 until his

Crimson Christ Church

death in 1553 on Shangchuan Island off the coast of Canton. In the church, a stone slab marks his tomb, empty since his remains were transported to Goa in India. Granite tombstones from the Dutch era stand against the walls. A Dutch and British **cemetery** is to be found further down the hill.

The **Tugu Pengistiharn Kemerdekaan** (Proclamation of Independence Memorial) occupies a villa built in 1912, which was once the Malacca Club for British colonials and local planters. It was on the club's *padang* (playing field) that future Prime Minister Tunku Abdul Rahman announced in 1956 the success of his London negotiations. Nowadays, the memorial building shows films and displays documents tracing the campaign for independence. Opposite, on Padang Pahlawan (Bandar Hill), a sound-and-light show is held in the evenings.

The Proclamation of Independence Memorial is housed in a former colonial clubhouse

Heading back to the river, you will find one of Melaka's more recent additions, the **Maritime Museum**, housed in a model of the *Flor De La Mar*, a Portuguese ship laden with bullion and other valuables that sank off Melaka. Exhibits include models of ships that have called at the port over its long and glorious history.

Malay Sultanate Palace

The **Istana Kesultanan Melayu** (Malay Sultanate Palace) is a cultural museum standing amid elegant gardens north of the Porta de Santiago. Reconstructed from ancient prints, it is an approximate but noteworthy replica of Mansur Shah's grandiose hilltop residence, which is believed to have burned down in 1460.

Chinatown

The living history of Melaka is to be found among the Baba Nyonya community, the descendants of the original Chinese pioneers and entrepreneurs who married local Malay women in the old Straits Settlements – Melaka, Penang and Singapore.

The narrow streets of Melaka's **Chinatown**, just next to the river, resound with the past, especially the 19th century, when entrepreneurs from this community helped lift the local economy. Their contribution now stands among the houses along **Jalan Tun Tan Cheng Lock**, also known as 'Millionaires' Row'. This is a paradise for the hunter of antiques, filled with new and old Oriental treasures – porcelain, statues, jewellery, silverware and heavy 19th-century furniture. Head to Jalan Hang Jebat (formerly Jonker Street) for more browsing and bargains.

Baba Nyonya culture blends Chinese and Malay traditions

One of these mansions, at 50 Jalan Tun Tan Cheng Lock, is **Baba Nyonya Heritage Museum**, an amalgam of three houses belonging to one family. Built in 1896 by rubber planter Chan Cheng Siew, this house offers a vivid introduction to the life and culture of the Straits Chinese, as the Babas are also known. In a style best described as Chinese Palladian, with its neoclassical columns and heavy hardwood doors, the furnishings and decor bear witness to the great prosperity of Baba entrepreneurs. A member of the Chan family usually gives guided tours of the house, which last about 45 minutes, and will point out its finer points – the silks, filigree, silver ornaments, gleaming blackwood furniture inlaid with ivory or mother-of-pearl, and a monumental gilded teak staircase leading to the bedrooms on the upper floor. Also of note are the massive wooden lattice screens though which unmarried daughters were allowed to peep at their parents' guests in the drawing room.

Along Jalan Tokong and Jalan Tukang Emas are Chinese and Hindu temples and a Muslim mosque. The **Cheng Hoon Teng Temple** (Evergreen Cloud Temple), originally built in 1646 by 'Kapitan China' Lee Wei King, a fugitive from China, claims to be the oldest Chinese temple in Malaysia.

Dedicated to Kuan Yin, it is flamboyantly decorated with multicoloured birds and flowers of glass and porcelain. The bronze statue of Kwan Yin, the Goddess of Mercy, was brought back from India in the 19th century. The **Kampung Kling Mosque**, on Jalan Tokong (1748), has a multi-tiered roof with a watchtower-style minaret. The nearby **Sri Poyyatha Vinayagar Moorthi Temple** (1781), dedicated to the elephant god Ganesh, or Vinayagar, is also one of the oldest in the country. On Jalan Kampung Pantai is the **Mausoleum of Hang Jebat**, a 16th-century warrior who was killed unjustly in a duel of honour with his friend Hang Tuah, who has a well named after him at Kampung Duyong.

Baba Nyonya

The Baba Nyonya community of Melaka *(baba*, male, *nyonya*, female) demonstrates the Chinese genius for adapting to local circumstances without losing the essentials of their own culture. Their subtle blend of Chinese and Malay traditions began back in the 15th century, when the entourage of Princess Hang Li Po, daughter of the Emperor of China and betrothed to Mansur Shah of Melaka, intermarried with local gentry. Their numbers were boosted in subsequent centuries by the influx of merchants and entrepreneurs, largely from Fukien in southern China.

The Chinese talent for business made a cheerful union with the Malay taste for pleasure, culminating in the joyously ostentatious affluence of the 19th and early 20th centuries. The Babas made their money from spices, rubber, timber and tin, and got their pleasure from gambling, a chew of betel nut, or an occasional pipe of opium. Their Nyonyas happily spent the family fortune on opulently furnished houses and in preparing elaborate trousseaus for their daughters.

Baba Nyonya cuisine is a triumphant synthesis of southern Chinese delicacies and the spice and pungency of Tamil-influenced Malay ingredients – garlic, red-hot chilli and rich coconut milk.

> Touching people on the head is considered rude, as the head is thought to be the most noble part of the body. Also, do not show anyone the soles of your feet, which are, conversely, the least dignified part of the body.

Outside the City Centre

Rather than drive around the sights away from the old city centre, you may prefer to relax and let a trishaw-driver find the way – and give you the bonus of his wry comments. Start perhaps with an evening ride past the open-air restaurants on Jalan Taman, better known as **Glutton's Corner**. Until the recent land reclamation for new housing developments, these Malay, Chinese and Tamil Indian eating places bordered the seafront, but the cuisine (the most notable dish being the spicy *mee hoon* noodles) has not changed.

Bukit Cina

Inland, the hillside provides a Chinese cemetery for more than 12,000 graves, mostly horseshoe-shaped tombs. At the top of the hill you will see foundations of the 16th-century Portuguese Franciscan monastery and get a splendid view over the town to the Melaka Straits. The gaudy red, gold and white **Sam Po Kong Temple** stands at the foot of Bukit Cina, honouring Cheng Ho, the eunuch admiral who in 1409 opened up Melaka to Chinese trade. Nearby is the **Perigi Raja** (Sultan's Well) dug in the 15th century for Princess Hang Li Po, whom the Emperor of China had given as a bride to Mansur Shah. Its pure waters were subsequently protected by Dutch fortifications.

➤ The Portuguese Settlement

A short drive some 3km (2 miles) south of the town centre along Jalan Parameswara takes you to the heart of this little Eurasian community, peopled by descendants of the Portuguese colonists. In the area around Jalan d'Albuquerque and

Dataran Portugis (Portuguese Square), the houses look no different from those in the rest of Melaka, but you may hear snatches of *Cristao,* a 16th-century Portuguese dialect. The restaurants on and off the square serve good seafood, though over the centuries the Portuguese cuisine has taken on a spicy Asian flavour. The community worships at the simple, unassuming **St Peter's Catholic Church**, where Easter is an especially big event, attracting many Indians, Chinese and Malay non-Catholics to the great, candlelit procession.

The Coast Roads

It is worth taking a ride north along the Jalan Tengkera coast road to visit some of the picturesque fishing villages. On the way, take a look at the fine three-tiered, Sumatra-style **Tranquerah Mosque** (1748), the burial place of Sultan Hussain Shah of Johor, who negotiated with Raffles the British rights

Portuguese descendants still speak Cristao, an antiquated language

to Singapore. You will find good crab and shrimp at the fishing village of **Pantai Kundor**. Further north, **Tanjung Bidara**, 35km (20 miles) from Melaka, has a hotel resort and some pleasant tree-shade on the beach for picnics.

Some 8km (5 miles) south of Melaka, you can take a boat at Umbai out to **Pulau Besar**, which has white sandy beaches, a jungle offering pleasant walks and a recently opened resort.

Penang

On the northeast coast of **Penang** (Pulau Pinang, meaning Betel Nut Island), George Town is the draw to Penang state, with rich colonial and historic roots amid the clutter of a market and commercial town. (The city is often referred to simply as 'Penang'.) Its narrow streets and busy thoroughfare add to the adventure, with its Chinese history reflected in the shophouses and older hotels. Entry points to the island are by road and rail, a ferry journey across the Selat Selatan from the industrial town of Butterworth, or by way of the 7-km (4½-mile) drive over the Penang Bridge, which provides wonderful views of the harbour. Flights, including international arrivals, land at the Bayan Lepas International Airport, which is 18km (11 miles) south of George Town. Taxis

A minaret in George Town

to the city are available to hire at the airport.

Most of the activity in Penang is in the city, but it is also possible to relax at a beach-side resort or to flee the heat by taking the railway link to the top of Penang Hill. You can step back into the island's history amid the colonial buildings, Chinese temples and shophouses. Delicious food and great shopping add to Penang's charm.

Penang Clock Tower

Under the British, Penang was named Prince of Wales Island, and the capital took its name from the son of King George III. Nowadays, Penang has the second largest economy among the states of Malaysia, with a population of just over one million. It is also the centre for the country's electronics industry. The tidal waves of Boxing Day 2004 swept a number of victims from the island's coast, although the damage wrought was considerably less than in other affected countries.

George Town

Today, **George Town**, is a blend of historic buildings and modern skyscrapers. The contrast is striking. Move from the rich, scented air surrounding the Chinese temples to such modern buildings as the 65-storey **Komtar** – or Tun Abdul Razak Complex – a government, shopping and entertainment centre.

Old Centre

One of the joys of touring George Town's historic section is the opportunity to cover many of the sites in this compact area by foot, and the best place to begin your tour is the main ferry terminal at **Weld Quay**. Along the foreshore there is the Kampung Ayer, or Chinese Water Village, better known as the **Clan Piers**, a hamlet of houses on stilts, joined by wooden walkways over the water and inhabited by 2,000 boatmen and fishing families, each group belonging to a different clan.

At the other end of Pengkalan Weld, opposite the Tourist Office, is the **Jam Besar** (Penang Clock Tower), built to mark Queen Victoria's Diamond Jubilee, and presented to the town in 1897. The tower is just over 18m (60ft) high, one foot for each year of Victoria's rule at the time of her Jubilee.

Across the road is **Fort Cornwallis** (named after Charles Cornwallis, Governor General of India), which marks the spot where Captain Light arrived on 17 July 1786. The greenery of the park and gardens surrounds the fortifications, which were originally made of wood and rebuilt in 1810. The cannons on the ramparts were never fired by the British in defence of the harbour. The oldest cannon is the **Seri Rambai**; originally given to the Sultan of Johor by the Dutch, it was transported to Penang in the 17th century aboard a British steamer of the same name. If you see flowers in the gun's barrel, it is likely to be an offering from a childless woman hoping for fertility, which the cannon is said to be able to bestow.

Light in the Jungle

On the northeast corner of the waterfront, Kedah Point marks the spot where the Penang settlement's founder Francis Light *(see page 22)* is said to have hit upon a cunning method of getting the surrounding jungle cleared to make way for the town. He loaded a cannon with Spanish silver dollars, fired them into the forest, and invited local labourers to hack their way through the undergrowth to get to the money.

Jin Tun Syed Sheh Barakhbah (also known as the Esplanade) runs between the waterfront and the Padang before the fort. This area is lined with handsome, 19th-century colonial government buildings, their brilliant white highly evocative of the era in which they were built. The British worshipped in **St George's Church** (1818) on Lebuh Farquhar. It is the oldest Anglican church in Southeast Asia. In the nearby cemetery, set among frangipani trees, is the **grave of Francis Light**, who died from malaria in 1794, only eight years after the start of his

Francis Light, founder of Penang

Penang adventure. There are many other graves, their tombstones revealing the hardships of the town's history.

Francis Light's statue stands at the entrance of the **Penang Museum** at the corner of Lebuh Light and Lebuh Farquhar. In fact, as no photograph of Light himself existed, the sculpture is a likeness made from a portrait of his son, William (who founded the city of Adelaide in Australia). The museum is housed in what was the Penang Free School. Founded in 1816, it was the first English-language school in Southeast Asia. There is a fine collection of historical memorabilia, old paintings, etchings and a 19th-century Chinese bridal chamber. Also on show is one incongruous exhibit left by the Royal Air Force: a bronze bust of the German Kaiser

Wilhelm II. The Penang Gallery at the Dewan Sri Pinang in Lebuh Light displays batik paintings, oils, graphics and Chinese ink drawings.

One of the great monuments from George Town's colonial days is the **Eastern & Oriental Hotel** at 10–12 Lebuh Farquhar. Even if you are not staying in one of the hotel's grand old rooms – where Rudyard Kipling and Somerset Maugham both stayed – do at least take a drink in the venerable 1885 Bar, whose name commemorates the year of the hotel's founding. The E & O is actually a fusion of two separate hotels: the Eastern, facing the Esplanade, and the Oriental, facing the sea. It was the brainchild of Martin and Tigran Sharkie, Armenian brothers who also created the famous Raffles Hotel in Singapore. Restored to its former splendour, it is now linked to a select group of hotels in Southeast Asia and Indochina. In the evening, sit by the pool overlooking the wide waters and dream of the days of the Empire.

Chinatown

The heartland of George Town's **Chinatown** is centred on **Lebuh Chulia** and **Lebuh Campbell**, both of which run off the city's main commercial thoroughfare of Jalan Penang. Here, amid a sea of two-storey shophouses and busy lanes, wares spill out, competing for space and the attention of shoppers. It is also an area favoured by backpackers, lured by cheap hotels and restaurants and the chance of purchasing discounted air tickets. You will be able to find good leather and canvas-wear for jungle treks on Campbell and Chulia streets. Here also are the betting shops, ancient bar-

Chinese immigrants arriving in Malaysia in the 19th century fell under the protection and control of clan associations, similar in function to medieval European guilds.

ber shops and stores offering exotic medicines.

Wander around the neighbourhood's back streets to admire the beautifully kept residential houses, many with elegantly carved teak window screens and doorways and handsome gold-and-black lacquered name plates. The more flamboyant are the **Clan Houses**, bulwarks of community solidarity. They combine temples for ancestral worship with meeting halls to settle local problems – housing, jobs, medical care, help for orphans and discreetly handled intra-community crime.

A Chinese Clan House

Off Lebuh Cannon – so called because of the holes made in the road surface here by cannonballs fired during the Great Penang Riot of 1867 – and through a laneway is the **Khoo Kongsi** (clan house of the family Khoo). Approach it via a narrow alley near the intersection of Jalan Acheh and Lebuh Pitt. Inside is an image of the clan's patron, Tua Sai Yeah, a renowned general of the Ch'in dynasty (221–7BC). Other houses nearby date back to the mid-19th century. The ornate ancestral temple **Leong San Tong** stands opposite a smaller hall used for open-air Chinese opera and theatre. To the left is a shrine to the God of Prosperity and to the right is the hall of *sinchoo* (soul-tablets), gold plaques honouring clan dignitaries and simpler wooden panels for more humble clan members.

The **Cheong Fatt Tze Mansion** on Lebuh Leith, built around 1860 by Thio Thaw Siat, a Chinese businessman, is considered one of the best examples of 19th-century Chinese architecture in Penang. Restored to its former glory, this 38-room, five-courtyard house gained UNESCO World Heritage Site status in 2000 and is now a boutique hotel. Tours are conducted twice a day.

The busiest public temple in Penang is the **Kuan Yin Teng Temple**, on Lebuh Pitt (Jalan Masjid Kapitan Kling), near St George's Church. Dedicated to the Goddess of Mercy, who has benevolent powers and is identified with the Indian Boddhisattva of Fertility, it draws both the rich and poor to pay respect and is popular with newly-wed couples. The shrine is protected by two stone lions at the entrance and guardian dragons on the roof. The atmosphere is heavy with the scent of burning joss-sticks mixed with the aroma of flowers, scented oils, fruits, cakes and roast chicken, offered on the altars to help solve family problems. This deity forms a bridge between traditional Chinese beliefs and Buddhism.

On the same street is the **Kapitan Kling Mosque**, the state's oldest mosque, built in 1800 for Muslim Indian soldiers. The **Sri Mariamman Temple** on Lebuh Queen (which runs parallel to Lebuh Pitt) was built in 1883 and is the oldest Hindu temple in Penang. Vividly decorated, it is dedicated to Lord Subramaniam, the son of Shiva and destroyer of evil, who is the focus of worship during the Thaipusam festival held in the early months of the year.

Beyond the City Centre

The famous **flea market** is now located at **Lorong Kulit** (literally Skin Lane), near the city's stadium. Here you can wade through mountains of old clothes, jewellery, household utensils, clocks, dolls, ornaments, old coins and all the bric-a-brac of an Oriental bazaar.

The other main sights of interest outside downtown George Town are Penang Hill and the Botanical Gardens. The drive out along **Jalan Sultan Ahmad Shah** takes you past the rubber magnates' huge neo-Gothic and Palladian mansions, built during the boom that lasted through World War I.

The Buddhist **Wat Chayamangkalaram monastery**, on Lorong Burma, is famous for its 33-m (108-ft) long reclining Buddha. The site for the temple was given to the community by Queen Victoria in 1845. The gigantic *naga* serpents, mystical creatures linking earth to heaven, are the balustrades at the entrance to the meditation hall.

Further west, away from the temple, you'll find the **Botanical Gardens**. The 30-hectare (74-acre) garden was created in 1844 as a tribute to Charles Curtis, its superintendent, who collected botanical specimens from the nearby hills. Leaf monkeys and long-tailed macaques are among the wildlife. One is cautioned about eating food openly, as the monkeys are likely to view this as an invitation to dine with you.

Naga, or serpent guardian, at Wat Chayamangkalaram

Jalan Dato Keramat, then Jalan Air Itam, lead west of town to the **Penang Hill**, 830m (2,722ft) above sea level, which served as a colonial hill station at the turn of the century, and is now popular as a weekend excursion for locals. Take a delightfully slow ride on the funicular railway (built in 1923) past bungalows and villas set amid handsome gardens for panoramic views of the island. Day-trippers wander along the canopy walk and trails through dense groves of bamboo to catch views of flora and wildlife. Birdwatchers look out for blue-tailed bee-eaters, sunbirds and spider-hunters.

Above the small town of Air Itam stands the **Kek Lok Si** (Temple of Paradise). It was founded by Abbot Beow Lean, a Chinese Buddhist priest from Fujian province in China who arrived in Penang in 1887. The temple's construction began in 1890 and took 20 years to complete. The centrepiece is the

Outside the Kek Lok Si Temple

seven-tiered **Pagoda of a Million Buddhas**, which is 30m (98ft) high and dedicated to Tsi Tsuang Wang. The pagoda is actually a blend of three architectural styles, a Chinese octagonal base, a Thai central core and a Burmese peak. At the **Tortoise Pond**, visitors feed the creatures with vegetables and 'tortoise biscuits'. Boulders on the grounds are covered with Chinese calligraphy of Buddhist and Confucian texts. Inside the shrine are statues of the Laughing Buddha, radiating happiness; Sakyamuni Buddha, incarnation of the faith's founder; and Kuan Yin, the Goddess of Mercy.

Around The Island

Away from George Town's hectic, bustling streets and midday heat, there is the chance to explore the remainder of the island. A tour around the island – about 74km (46 miles) – will give you the best chance to meet the Malay population, who live largely in the rural *kampungs* and fishing villages. The island is a blend of hilly

An offering in Kek Lok Si

rainforest and occasional plantations of rubber, oil palms, pepper, nutmeg, cloves and other spices. An island tour can be accomplished in just a day, although overnight accommodation away from the beach resorts is limited.

About 15km (9½ miles) northwest of George Town are the resorts of **Batu Ferringhi** (Foreigner's Rock), with sandy beaches and rows of luxury hotels offering waterskiing, sailing, windsurfing, horse riding and other sports. There are also small inns and motels in the vicinity for travellers on a budget. Though sandy, the beaches may prove disappointing to those who have travelled on the northeastern coastline.

On a journey around the island, potential locations for stopovers are **Sungei Pinang** and **Pantai Aceh**, small Chinese villages reached by turning west off the main road. For fishing and snorkelling, stop at Teluk Bahang and hire a boat out to **Muka Head** on the island's northwest tip. In the south, **Batu Maung** offers scenic views and seafood restaurants, including one built on stilts over the water.

Alternatively, you could trek through the **Penang National Park**. The forest reserve covers some 20 sq km (8 sq miles) of the island's northwest corner. With only camping available as accommodation and vehicles denied access, the reward comes in sighting wildlife like wild pigs, leopard-cats, slow loris, flying lemurs, leaf monkeys, macaques and black squirrels. The landscape is dotted with granite outcrops.

Near Teluk Bahang's town centre are the **Tropical Spice Garden** and **Penang Cultural Centre**; the latter features art and crafts and music and dance, as well as traditional architecture from elsewhere in Malaysia. At the southern end of Teluk Bahang village is the **Penang Butterfly Farm**, which has hundreds of different specimens fluttering around a netted enclosure of landscaped gardens.

A **tropical fruit farm**, just 8km (5 miles) from Teluk Bahang, has cultivated 140 types of exotic fruit trees on its 10 hectares (25 acres) since opening in 1992. Birdwatchers usually gather around **Genting**, about 3km (2 miles) from Balik Pulau, one of the world's largest nesting grounds for bee-

A Malay kampung house made of wood, with a zinc roof

eaters of all varieties – blue tailed, blue-throated, chestnut-headed and others flock here in their hundreds.

As the road turns north again past the airport at Bayan Lepas, watch out for signs to the **Snake Temple**, more correctly known as, the Temple of the Azure Cloud. Fifteen kilometres (9 miles) south from George Town, it was built in 1850 as a dedication to a Chinese monk, Chor Soo Kong, who gained fame through his ability to heal. After the temple was invaded by Wagler's vipers, it was decided they were incarnations of the monk and accorded sacred status.

> **Although the snakes in the Temple of the Azure Cloud are poisonous, they are supposedly doped into a harmless state by the incense smoke. A few are said to have had their teeth pulled, and the monks will be happy to drape them around the shoulders of a camera-ready tourist.**

North to Langkawi

Part of an archipelago of some 100 islets, the pretty resort island of Langkawi lies just south of the sea border to Thailand and, with its myriad hotels and motels, is increasingly seen as a regional resort option. If you are travelling there by road (rather than taking a flight from KL), ferries leave from Kuala Perlis and Kuala Kedah. There are daily ferries from Penang and a twice-weekly ferry to and from Thailand's Phuket Island. There are also international flights to Langkawi from London Heathrow, Singapore and Kansai Airport in Japan.

The Kedah–Perlis Coast Road

From Butterworth, the road stretching north into **Kedah State** heads into the rice bowl of Malaysia. Seas of green spread out on either side of the highway as it passes by the **Lembah Bujang** (Bujang Valley).

In the valley is an archaeological site that possibly dates back to a 5th-century Hindu kingdom called Langkasuka. The Indian traders may have used the city as an entrepot with China. Buddhist temples have also been uncovered in the area.

Archaeologists are still uncovering remains on the southern slopes of **Gunung Jerai** (Kedah Peak). At 1,200m (3,936ft), this is the highest peak in Kedah. The Sungei Teroi Forest Recreation Park is to be found halfway up the mountain.

Via the towns of Sungai Petani and Bedong, a left turn takes you to **Merbok** to visit the **Candi Bukit Batu Pahat** (Temple of Chiselled Stone Hill). This is one of the 10th-century temples now reconstructed in the Lembah Bujang and possibly built by representatives of the South Indian Pallava dynasty before the 7th century BC. More artefacts, ceramics, *lingams* (phallic symbols), stone caskets, and gold and silver Shiva symbols are on show at Merbok's **Archaeological Museum**.

Lying beyond Gunung Jerai are rice fields fed by the Muda River, which extend up to Perlis in the north and along the coastline from Penang to Langkawi. The Kedah State capital, **Alor Setar**, is the last stop before the Thai border, and its history is a sad catalogue of invasion and subjugation, mostly by the Siamese (Thais). In the city centre is the traditional *padang* (square), here dominated by the Crown of Kedah monument. The **Masjid Zahir**, built in 1912, stands on the square's western side. Its Moorish architecture is highlighted at night by myriad small lights. Nearby is the **Balai Besar**, built in 1898 in the Siamese style for royal audiences. Opposite the Masjid Zahir is the octagonal **Balai Nobat**, a tower where the royal instruments – drums, flutes and gongs – are stored. *Nobat*, the royal orchestra, plays during royal ceremonies; however, the tower is not open to the public. The **State Museum**, about 15 minutes by car just north of the city, was built in 1736, and is worth a visit for its collection of *Bunga Mas* and *Bunga Perak* (flowers made of real gold and silver), which were sent to the ancient court of Siam as tribute.

The nearby port of **Kuala Kedah** is a departure point for ferries to Langkawi; you can see the remains of an 18th-century fort and sample some of northern Malaysia's best seafood.

Malaysia's smallest state, **Perlis**, also marks a change of scenery, from the flat rice lands to solitary limestone outcrops, many containing subterranean caves. The main towns are **Arau**, the royal town, and **Padang Besar**, where the Malaysian and Thai railways meet. From **Kuala Perlis**, south of the state capital, **Kangar**, it is a one-hour ferry journey to Langkawi. You can also buy cheap fruit at the local market.

Pulau Langkawi

The Langkawi island group, a cluster of more than 100 islands, some of which disappear under the high tide, have been a focal

Pantai Cenang at Langkawi offers beach-front accommodation

Lake of the Pregnant Maiden

point in Malaysia's tourism promotion. But tourism in the area is centred on **Pulau Langkawi** and its array of some 80 holiday resorts and hotels. For the ferry traveller, **Kuah** is your arrival point, while those coming by air will land at the international airport, 18km (11 miles) northwest of the town. Kuah has some good Chinese, Thai, Indian and Malay restaurants and shops selling a range of goods at duty-free rates. Kuah's town square is dominated by a sculpture of a giant eagle (*langkawi* means red eagle in Malay). Next to the square is a theme park with 20 hectares (50 acres) of landscaped gardens.

To discover Langkawi's 80km (50 miles) of roads, it's possible to hire four-wheel-drive and standard cars, but many find bicycles and motorcycles the most attractive way to explore the island and reach the more secluded beaches. Swimmers should be careful of powerful currents at most of the beaches.

Most accommodation is located near Kuah town or within easy reach of the international airport. The main resorts near Kuah include the **Sheraton Perdana**, **Four Seasons** and **Tanjung Rhu Resort**, while those closer to the airport, on the island's southwestern tip, include the **Pelangi Beach Resort**, **Casa del Mar**, **Bon Ton Resort** and the **Awana Porto Malai**. However, there are plenty of beach chalets and huts located at beaches around the island.

Development at **Pantai Cenang** is among the most extensive on the island. An aquarium here, **Underwater World**, is reputed to be one of the largest in Asia, with more than 5,000 marine and freshwater fish. **Tasik Dayang Bunting** (Lake of the Pregnant Maiden), the largest freshwater lake in the Langkawi islands is associated with the fable of a Kedah princess who drank the lake's water and became pregnant.

On the northern cape of Pulau Langkawi is **Tanjung Rhu** (Casuarina Bay). From here a boat journey is the only way to reach the **Gua Cerita** (Cave of Legends), inscribed with writings from the Koran.

Other beaches to visit include **Pantai Kok**, **Pantai Tengah**, **Datai** and **Burau Bay**. Historical romantics may be interested to know that the islands were a favoured hideaway for the many pirates who preyed on ships in the Melaka Straits.

Adventurous beach-goers might be interested in a **jungle trek** across the middle of the island. Guided tours can be arranged for the hilly **Gunung Raya** and **Machinchang Forest Reserves**, where a wide array of wildlife and birdlife can be seen. One of the easier walks takes you over to the **Durian Perangin Waterfall**.

At the **Pulau Singa Besar Wildlife Sanctuary**, 45 minutes south of Kuah by boat, in 640 hectares (1,581 acres) of proctected land, you'll find monkeys, mouse-deer, iguanas and peacocks, as well as a fossil park and an astronomy centre.

Other sites include a **Craft Cultural Complex** on the northern coast of Langkawi near Teluk Yu; and, near the airport, the **Atma Alam Batik Art Village**, a centre showcasing batik artists at work.

> **The absence of a detailed, legitimate history of Langkawi Island has led some to cultivate its mythology. One fable surrounds the death of Mahsuri. Her tomb, 12km (7 miles) west of Kuah, set amid a picturesque garden, pays tribute to a woman wrongly executed for adultery more than 200 years ago. As legend has it, she bled white blood, a testament to her innocence, and in her dying words cursed the island for seven generations.**

THE EAST COAST AND JOHOR

Malaysia's less-visited east coast offers the visitor a slower pace, set against the beauty of the region's beaches and the richness of its forests. The region covers four states – **Kelantan**, **Terengganu**, **Pahang** and **Johor** – with most road traffic plying the coastal road between Kota Bharu, close to the Thai border, and Johor Bahru, just a causeway's distance from Singapore. Historically resistant to many of the major changes in the rest of Malaysia, the region has been able to maintain its authentic Malay culture and Islamic traditions.

> Traditional handicrafts, including the making of spinning tops, kites, silverware, baskets and batik, are still practised in many of the rural *kampung* in Kelantan and Terengganu.

The east coast's beaches are less developed and offer opportunities for snorkelling and diving. Wildlife enthusiasts can enter the forests for jungle trekking and adventure travel. The region also offers the chance to see leatherback turtles coming to lay their eggs at Cherating near Kuantan; and to view the craftsmen at Kuala Terengganu, whose boating abilities are legendary.

Economic growth and prosperity – recently through the discovery of oil offshore from Terengganu – has led to more hotels opening, offering a wider range of accommodation at competitive rates.

Kelantan

White sandy beaches stretch north from the state capital, Kota Bharu, to the Thai border. Buddhist temples close to the capital hark back to the time when Kelantan was under the influence of Siamese kings. The British colonial influence here, which came into being in a 1909 agreement with

Siam, only lasted three decades before their defeat by the Japanese in World War II. Kelantan's isolation, as well as its embrace of Islam in the 17th century, kept British colonialism and economic change at bay during the 19th century and enabled this cradle of Malay culture to remain intact.

Here you will see soaring decorative kites as well as the *wayang kulit* (shadow puppet shows), a throwback to when Kelantan was influenced by the kingdom of Funan in Indochina some 2,000 years ago.

Known as the 'Land of Lightning' – due to the heavy storms during the wet season of November to February – Kelantan's gateway is Kota Bharu, just 40 minutes by air from Kuala Lumpur and only 30km (19 miles) from the Thai border. To the south, where towns dot the main highway, are points of access to the many beaches and fishing villages, which are at the heart of the region's economy and culture.

Boat-building is one of many traditional crafts practised in Kelantan

Kota Bharu

Set upon the banks of the Kelantan River, Kota Bahru's key attractions are close to the **Pasar Besar** (Central Market) on Jalan Doktor. Here rows of food and farm produce resemble works of art, with vegetables, fruit and meat on the ground level and kitchenware, baskets and other goods on the floors above.

The **Buluh Kubu Bazaar** is good for bargain-hunters seeking T-shirts or silverware. Silversmiths are also to be found on **Jalan Sultanah Zainab**, while batik and other cottage-industry goods are found over the Jalan Wakat Mek Zainab bridge. The **night market**, near Pasar Besar, will prove worthwhile evening entertainment and give you a chance to savor Kelantanese food.

At sundown, riverside restaurants also come to life near to **Padang Merdeka** (Independence Square), now an open park area for recreation but once the town's fresh produce market.

Fresh produce at Kota Bharu

Merdeka Square was the site where the body of slain Malay warrior Tok Janggut (Father Long Beard), who led a rebellion against the British in the early years of the century, was exhibited in 1915. The Declaration of Independence was read here on 31 August 1957.

Across the square is the **War Museum**, housed in the building once used by the Japanese Army as their headquarters; it's the oldest brick building in town, built in 1912. Next door is the

Batik-making involves colourful and intricate design

Muzium Islam (Islamic Museum), and the ornate **Masjid Negeri** (State Mosque) beyond.

The **Istana Jahar** (Royal Customs Museum) was built in 1887, with additions by Sultan Muhamad IV in the early years of the 20th century. The **Istana Balai Besar** (Palace with the Large Audience Hall) was built in 1840 under Sultan Muhamad II and is now only opened for ceremonial occasions (closed to the public). Inside is a throne room, royal furniture and a royal barge, used only once in 1900.

On the other side of town, along Jalan Hospital, near the Tourist Information Centre, is the **Kelantan State Museum**, displaying rural Malay artwork and earthenware pots. The best view of living Malaysian culture is to be seen at the **Gelanggang Seni** (Culture Centre) on Jalan Mahmood opposite the Perdana Hotel, with performances that include *wayang kulit*, *main gasing* (top spinning) and *silat* (self defence), except on Fridays and during Ramadan.

Around Kota Bharu

Within just a few kilometres of Kota Bharu, you can find master silversmiths and expert batik-makers, but the maze of country lanes around the town could make it difficult to find the *kampung* communities where the artisans still ply their traditional skills. A guide can be recommended by the Tourist Information Centre.

Kelantan's silversmiths use two techniques, the 'filigree' and '*repoussé*', and items range from the purely ornamental to the functional. Silver-craft factories can be visited at **Kampung Sireh**, along Jalan Sultanah Zainab, **Kampung Marak** and **Kampung Badang**, as well as on the road to Pantai Cahaya Bulan (PCB). Also on the way to PCB, you can see the skill and beauty of *kain songket*, richly woven materials of gold and silver thread, at **Kampung Penambang**. Songket was the product of the region's early trade with China (silk)

Preparing to fly a colourful kite or *wau*

and India (gold and silver thread). Indigenous to Kelantan, batik-makers are found throughout the state, but the bigger factories are to be found at **Kampung Puteh**, **Kubur Kuda** and **Kampung Badang**.

When visiting a place of worship remember to dress in an appropriately dignified manner. Note that you must also slip off your shoes before entering a mosque or a Hindu temple.

Kite-makers also practise their age-old skills throughout the region, and while tradition would have the art passed from father to son, many fear the younger generation now lacks the patience to carry out the skilled handiwork required.

One of the oldest mosques in Malaysia is found at **Nilam Puri**. It was dismantled and taken from a site closer to the river at Kampung Laut in 1968, after repeated flooding. The mosque was built entirely without the use of nails. It is now a centre for religious studies, but non-Muslims may not enter.

Kelantan's ancient links with Thailand are evident in the number of **Thai Buddhist Temples** you will see half-hidden among the groves of palm and laurel, rising above the rice paddies. North of the estuary of the Kelantan River near **Tumpat** (12 km/7 miles from town) is one of the most important of these temples, **Wat Phothivihan**, which is noted for its 40-m (130-ft) reclining Buddha. At **Kampung Perasit**, south of Kota Bharu, is **Wat Putharamaram**.

A significant landmark of World War II can be visited at **Sabak Beach**, 13km (8 miles) northwest of the Kota Bharu, near the mouth of the Kelantan River. Here is the site of the first Japanese assault in the Pacific War, just over an hour before Pearl Harbor was bombed (*see page 28*). Jutting out of the sandy beach in the pleasant shade of palm and casuarina trees stands a crumbling bunker that the Indian artillery defended to the last man.

The Beaches

Kelantan's white sandy beaches are easily reached from Kota Bharu and provide plenty of opportunities for a pleasant swim. Most popular is **Pantai Cahaya Bulan,** or Moonlight Beach. It was previously known as Pantai Cinta Berahi, the Beach of Passionate Love, a somewhat incongruous name in this strict Muslim region where *khalwat,* or close proximity, is prohibited. It is just 10km (6 miles) north of the town, one reason why it is so popular during weekends and school holidays.

Pantai Seri Tujuh (Beach of the Seven Lagoons), about 7km (4 miles) from Kota Bharu, is the venue for the International Kite Festival and lies on the border with Thailand.

To the south, **Pantai Irama** (Melody Beach) is some 25km (16 miles) from Kota Bharu; it is one of the most beautiful along the entire coast. On the journey to Terengganu is **Pantai Bisikan Bayu** (Beach of the Whispering Breeze, also known as Pantai Dalam Rhu). Stop off at the fishing village of **Semerak,** 19km (12 miles) from Pasir Puteh, where you can buy excellent seafood for a barbecue on the beach.

Terengganu

A coast of sandy beaches along the 225km (140 miles) of landfall facing the South China Sea, not to mention myriad offshore islands and hinterland forests near Tasik (Lake) Kenyir, are the draw to Terengganu. The wealth from offshore oil discoveries in recent years has buoyed the state, something you'll see reflected in the skyline and busy traffic of the capital, Kuala Terengganu. So far the economic gains have failed to detract from the town's relaxed charm. The main options for travelling to Terengganu are direct flights from KL or interstate buses to Kuala Terengganu, which is generally the starting point for a trip to the island resorts or to Tasik Kenyir National Park.

The Islands

The islands off Terengganu's north coast are accessible from both Kuala Terengganu – where most resort companies have booking offices – or by way of the fishing village of **Kuala Besut**, 45km (28 miles) south of Kota Bharu, which is the departure point to Pulau Perhentian's islands. Before leaving Kuala Besut, you could visit **Bukit Keluang**, just on the coast, for watersports, with caves easily reached by walkways.

The islands of **Pulau Perhentian Kecil** and **Pulau Perhentian Besar** are reached after a 21-km (13-mile) journey which takes up to two hours. The islands' main reputations lie in their being lush and tropical, with clear blue waters and coral reefs protected as part of Malaysia's marine parks. On both islands accommodation ranges from lavish resorts to chalets or huts.

South from Pulau Perhentian Besar lies **Pulau Redang**, some 50km (31 miles) off the coast. Its nine islands make up

Lake Kenyir, Terengganu

the largest of Terengganu's archipelagoes. It is also developing quickly and is strongly promoted by travel agents in Kuala Terengganu, but there is still the promise of crystal-clear waters for scuba diving. The journey to the islands takes two hours from the village of Merang (not to be confused with the town of Marang further south). There are also resorts on **Pulau Lang Tengah**, just west of the Redang Islands. Boats take 45 minutes to reach the island from Merang.

Kuala Terengganu

The lively state capital of **Kuala Terengganu**, bordered by the Terengganu River and the South China Sea, is the largest town

Sunset at Kuala Terengganu

in the state and has progressed from a sleepy fishing village to a bustling, colourful centre. Aside from the beautiful **Masjid Tengku Tengah Zaharah**, 4½km (3 miles) out of town, most sites of interest are along the town's waterfront. The mosque, built on an estuary of the Ibai River, gives the illusion that it is floating on water.

Back in town, a waterfront stroll leads through **Chinatown** on Jalan Bandar. The old terraced buildings on both sides of the road create an attractive sense of timelessness even as the betting shops do a lively afternoon trade. Jalan Bandar leads you to the **Pasar Besar**

Kedai Payang (Central Market), a multi-level complex attached to a car park, with a fruit, vegetable and fish market on the ground floor and local textiles and handicrafts above.

The 200-m (656-ft) high **Bukit Puteri**, a hill just beyond the market, has an old fort dating from 1831–76 that was used in a local civil war. Its view overlooks the **Istana Maziah**, the sultan's palace, built in 1897, which is not open to the public. Behind the palace, the **Masjid Zainal Abidin** was originally built of timber between 1793 and 1808. It was rebuilt in stone in 1852 and renovated in 1972.

A short river cruise from the jetty, **Pulau Duyung Besar** is a little island of boat-builders, whose reputations extend far beyond Malaysia. The clients who buy their hardwood craft are more likely to be wealthy American and Australian yachtsmen than local people.

Several other attractions are located outside the town. Opposite Pulau Sekati, 5km (3 miles) from town – but also accessible from the river – is the **Terengganu State Museum**, in a traditionally styled complex of four blocks housing 10 galleries at Bukit Losong. The largest state museum in Malaysia, its galleries are dedicated to maritime exhibits, traditional architecture, Islamic arts, textiles, crafts, and royal regalia. For local silk weaving, try the **Sutera Semai Centre** at Chendering, 6km (3 miles) from Kuala Terengganu, where visitors can witness different stages of silk-making and batik-painting. Also on offer is *songket*, woven with silver and gold threads, and brassware.

Around Kuala Terengganu

Fifty-five kilometres (34 miles) inland from Kuala Terengganu is the largest man-made lake in Southeast Asia, **Tasik Kenyir**, which was created by flooding the valley to construct the country's largest hydroelectric dam, completed in 1985. For the angler looking for freshwater fish, Tasik Kenyir National Park, covering an area of 37,000 hectares (91,400 acres) and 340 islands, is the place to go. An international fishing competition is even held here. Besides fishing, jet skiing, windsurfing, canoeing and jungle trekking are all available.

There are also several waterfalls, rapids and cascades within the lake region, including the **Sekayu Waterfalls**, just 56km (35 miles) west of Kuala Terengganu. After trekking through the rainforest, you can enjoy a swim in one of the many natural pools created among the rocks by the cascading river.

Marang is a fishing village 15km (9 miles) south of Kuala Terengganu. Here, and across the long wooden bridge at **Patah Malam**, you may see fishermen mending their nets in the shade of coconut palms. From Marang lies access to the island of **Pulau Kapas** which, though less than 2km (1 mile) in length, is considered one of the most pleasant islands on the east coast. There are several resorts and chalet accommodation on the island.

Save the Turtles

In the years before ecological awareness, many onlookers treated the turtles' rendezvous as a popular spectacle. Crowds gathered in festive mood to build campfires on the beach, dance to loud music, take pictures by blinding flashlight of the turtles' night-time egg laying, even ride the backs of the giant leatherbacks and poke open their heavy-lidded eyes. This irresponsibility almost put a stop to the natural phenomenon. The annual number of leatherbacks visiting Rantau Abang declined from about 2,000 in the 1950s to barely a few hundred by the end of the 1980s. At this point, the Malaysian fisheries department stepped in to protect the turtles. Authorities have banned the use of flash photography or flashlights, and visitors must stay 5m (15ft) from the turtles – although not everyone follows the guidelines. High tide at a full moon is the most likely time to sight a leatherback.

Rantau Abang

Rantau Abang's claim to fame comes from the giant leatherback turtles that visit the beaches to lay their precious eggs, as conservationists struggle to reverse the creatures' declining numbers. The beach attracts a variety of turtles, including the hawksbill, the common green and the olive ridley. Rantau Abang, 60km (38 miles) south of Kuala Terengganu, is one of only six places in the world visited by these turtles. During the months of May and September, a sanctuary extends 10km (6 miles) on either side of Rantau Abang. Special hatch-

Measuring a visiting leatherback

eries have been set aside, where the eggs are collected from the initial nest and reburied in a safe location. A Turtle Information Centre is located to the north of the village.

It is during the midnight to dawn hours that the female leatherbacks, up to 2½m (8ft) in length and weighing sometimes over 375kg (825lb), make their way up the beach. During daylight hours, the beach's sparkling waters and ambience are enough of a reason to visit.

Tanjung Jara and Points South

The highway south from Rantau Abang, heading towards Kuantan, the state capital of Pahang, passes through **Tanjung Jara**. Here, the award-winning accommodation of the beach resort contrasts with the rapid industrialisation from the offshore oil and gas exploration in the region. Further south is **Kuala Dungun**, which is predominantly Chinese in character and offers excellent cuisine. A boat can be hired from here to the island of **Pulau Tenggol**, 30km (18 miles) offshore, so you can go snorkelling among the angelfish. The centre of Terengganu's petroleum industry is **Kerteh**, with its refineries and gasworks. But there are some pretty beaches at the mouth of the Kerteh River nonetheless.

Pahang

The largest state in the peninsula also has the longest river, the 475-km (296-mile) long Pahang. Although its most famous sights lie far to the west in the Genting and Cameron Highlands, Pahang has its share of beach resorts, including the renowned Pulau Tioman (Tioman Island) in the far south (though access by sea is from the port of Mersing in Johor). The recently developed Endau Rompin National Park, straddling the border with Johor state, complements the better known Taman Negara in the far north, which has road access through the state capital Kuantan. Pahang's other natural beauties include Lake Chini.

The Coast

Just 47km (30 miles) from Kuantan is the beach resort area of **Cherating**, where Club Mediterranée set up its first resort in Asia. But Club Med is not alone along the beachfront. Other resorts in close proximity to the state's capital are located at **Balok Beach**. The Hyatt Hotel Kuantan has joined other resorts at the **Teluk Chempedak Beach**, only 5km (3 miles) out of the bustling city. The beautiful **Pelindung Beach** is just a short trek through the Teluk Chempedak Forest Reserve. From May to September, green turtles and the occasional giant leatherback may be seen under moonlit skies when they lay their eggs on the beach. At the **Beserah Beach**, also close to Kuantan, local fishermen still employ buffalo to pull the carts carrying their catch to the market. A batik factory and several cottage handicraft workshops here may disappoint the more sophisticated souvenir-hunter. You will find a pleasant beach nearby at **Batu Hitam**.

Kuantan

Kuantan township offers a wide range of hotels, a lively shopping and market quarter, and a quiet ambience next to the river where good food stalls are found. Built on the fortunes from tin mining, the capital is now a commercial centre for Pahang's oil, palm and other industries, and a key link in the East Coast petroleum and gas pipelines.

A peaceful vista in Cherating

You'll find an array of Chinese hotels, which, like Hotel Min Heng (1926) and the Tong Nam Ah Hotel, have interesting backgrounds. The Mega View Hotel near the river says it all in its name. But there are also several new hotels close to the river and in sight of the impressive **Masjid Negeri** (State Mosque), such as the Shahzan Inn. On the same street, Jalan Masjid, is the cultural centre (**Infokraf**), and just opposite is an open sports field. The area around Jalan A. Aziz and Jalan Besar is hectic with shops, wares and an occasional money-lender. The local village of **Selamat** is known for its fine *kain songket* silk brocade.

Just 25km (16 miles) northwest of Kuantan, **Gua Charah**, a cave temple, is built into one of the limestone outcrops surrounding the town. Inside the cave, known as the 'yawning skull cave', echoing with the sound of bats, a 9-m (29-ft) reclining Buddha is to be found among the illuminated shrines.

Pekan

The sleepy old royal capital of Pahang, 45km (28 miles) south of Kuantan, is still the sultan's official residence. Upstream on the Pahang River, the sultan's gleaming palace, **Istana Abu Bakar**, is set among immaculate green polo fields. Gilded and sapphire-blue domes grace two white marble **mosques** and the **Sultan's Mausoleum**. Nearby, the Victorian **State Museum** displays glories of the old sultanate and treasures from a Chinese junk salvaged from the South China Sea. The town also has a silk-weaving centre, located at **Kampung Pulau Keladi**, 5km (3 miles) from Pekan.

The golden-domed home of the Sultan of Pekan

Tasik Chini

Comprising a dozen beautiful lakes surrounded by forested hills, **Tasik Chini** is situated south of the Pahang River,

100km (60 miles) west of Kuantan. From August to September, much of the surface is covered by white lotus blossoms. The myth-shrouded lakes are said to be the home of giant snakes, dragons and other monsters, one of which, according to local myth, swam to the South China Sea and became Tioman Island. Archaeological explorations suggest there are ruins of a Khmer settlement beneath the surface. Outside lotus-blossom season, the lakes are still a delight to visit, with good fishing for the local *toman*. Members of the local Jakun tribe dwell on the lake's shore. It may be possible to pay a discreet visit to one of their hamlets, **Kampung Gumum**.

Tioman Island

The combination of first-rate resort facilities and magnificent natural beauty makes **Tioman Island** one of the finest in Asia. Preserved from logging, most of the rainforest has remained. A hilly ridge runs down the middle of the island at an altitude of 500m (1,640ft), rising at the southern end to two granite peaks – the Donkey's Ears. The taller of these, Mount Kajang, is 1,038m (3,405ft) high.

You can reach Tioman by flying from Kuantan or by taking the boat from the fishing village of Mersing in Johor. The 'slow boat' and the 'fast boat' both end up taking three to four hours.

On the island's west coast, you have the choice between the top-class **Berjaya Tioman Resort Hotel** and the more modest but comfortable guest-houses, chalets and simpler cabins on **Salang Beach** further north. Facilities around the main island port of **Tekek** include restaurants, diving shops and a golf course, where long-tailed macaques act as unofficial caddies who do not always give the ball back.

Most trips around the island are by boat, and the fishermen charge a reasonable fee. From Tekek, make the **jungle trek** over the hill to the east coast. Cool off on the way with a dip at the hilltop waterfall, then make your way down to the beach at **Juara**, a village serving excellent seafood and banana pancakes. Take another swim in the sea, and if you do not feel like trekking back, return to Tekek by boat.

Birdwatchers will see green pied imperial pigeons, bulbuls, frigate birds, sunbirds and flower-peckers. Characteristically for island forests, there are no large mammals.

Johor

Proximity to Singapore has added buoyancy to the economy of Johor, the peninsula's southernmost state, and also to that of its capital, Johor Bahru. Easy access from Singapore to east-coast resorts such as Desaru in the southeast and the islands offshore from Mersing has also led to the increased development of these destinations. Johor's links to Singapore have renewed and solidified its position as a guardian of Malay culture since it first provided a refuge in the 16th century for the banished royal court of Melaka. Johor offers travellers a wide range of opportunities for tourism, from shopping to motor racing, horse riding to water sports, and adventure travel to the Endau Rompin National Park, the relatively untouched forests at the border with Pahang.

The Endau-Rompin National Park

Straddling the border between Johor and Pahang, **Endau-Rompin National Park**'s 870 sq km (336 sq miles) of jungle and rivers is fast gaining a reputation among travellers as an alternative to the older Taman Negara. The park is home to tigers, elephants, wild boar and the largest surviving population of Sumatran rhinoceros in peninsular Malaysia. Other species to be found here include the *binturong* (bear cat) and the white-handed gibbon, the only ape species in the region. Among the birdlife are chirping drongos, hornbills and argus pheasants. The Endau-Rompin is also home to the Orang Asli of the Jakun tribe.

Much less developed than the parks of Sarawak and Sabah – and so far more pristine – Endau-Rompin offers a rare challenge to the adventurous traveller. Facilities for accommodation are limited to chalets, dormitories and three campsites in the park, located at **Batu Hampar**, **Upeh Guling** and **Buaya Sangkut**. You must employ a guide or go on a group tour.

From Johor Bahru, travel by the north–south highway to Keluang, and take a detour to Kahang town. From there, only a four-wheel-drive vehicle will take you along the 56-km (35-mile) jungle track to Kampung Peta, where there is a visitor centre and point of entry to the national park. Otherwise, you can get there via a three-hour boat journey from Felda Nitar II. There is controlled entry and quite strident regulations governing park usage and duration periods.

Following a river trail in the Endau-Rompin National Park

Desaru and the Islands North

The southeast corner of the peninsula was originally used for oil-palm plantations. Today, tourism drives the economy, and its high-class hotels share 25km (15 miles) of golden sands. **Desaru** is accessible by road by way of **Kota Tinggi**, or by following the coast road from Johor Bahru. If travelling through Kota Tinggi, it might be worthwhile making a stopover to see the spectacular **waterfall** at **Lombong**, 15km (9½ miles) north from the town centre. Desaru is 52km (32 miles) further east and is the first major beach resort outside Singapore. There are several top-end resorts and golf courses here, including the Desaru Golden Beach Hotel and the Desaru View Golf and Country Club, but budget travellers will also find reasonable value chalet accommodation available.

Off the coast from the resorts of **Mersing**, there are several islands – **Pulau Rawa**, **Pulau Tengah**, **Pulau Besar**, **Pulau Tinggi** and **Pulau Sibu** – offering white sandy beaches, coral reefs and budget accommodation. Boats can be hired from Mersing to take you out to one of the secluded islands.

Johor Bahru

Citizens of prosperous but staid Singapore cross the causeway to Johor's state capital to escape for the weekend and sample its lively nightlife, to shop, or to head further north. Outside the restaurants and malls, travellers can visit the sprawling **market**, and nearby along the **Lido Waterfront** take a look at the gleaming white marble of the **Sultan Abu Bakar Mosque**, the **Royal Museum** and the **Istana Gardens** of the old palace, with its Japanese tea house and a zoo put together from the sultan's private menagerie.

The neoclassical **Istana Besar Palace** is now used only for state ceremonies, the present-day sultans having moved up the coast to the modern **Istana Bukit Serene**, with a 32-m (104-ft) high tower. Other sights include the colonial-style clock tower overlooking the **Dataran Bandaraya** (City Square). The Johor Art Gallery, built in 1910 in a similar period style, exhibits clothing, weapons, currency and manuscripts, as well as examples of calligraphy and ceramic items, along with artworks.

North Towards Melaka

Two roads – Jalan Tun Dr Ismail and Jalan Tun Abdul Razak – lead northwards out of Johor Bahru to the west coast. Not far from Taman Tasik they merge into one in the direction of Ayer Hitam. Before heading towards Melaka, gourmets turn west at Skudai to the coast road and back south to **Kukup**, a fishing village 40km (25 miles) southwest of Johor Bahru.

Good visibility and thriving underwater life makes for great diving

At **Ayer Hitam**, a wide range of Chinese-style pottery is on display beside the fruit market, where there is an excellent selection of rambutans, pineapples and bananas, as well as locally-made nougat and fruit cakes. The market town of **Batu Pahat** also offers respectable Chinese restaurants. The town witnessed a historic Melaka naval victory over the Siamese fleet in 1456. The fishing port of **Muar** was of trading importance to the British in the 19th century, as can be seen in the graceful old neoclassical government offices. It was here that Australian troops made an heroic last stand against the Japanese advance on Singapore in January 1942.

SARAWAK & SABAH

A Dayak woman

From jungles to mountains, the states of Sarawak and Sabah offer enough adventure and natural beauty to make the journey across the South China Sea worthwhile. These sections of Borneo are sorely tried by the onslaughts of oil drilling, voracious logging of lucrative *belian* hardwood, and tourism itself. But images of cloud-engulfed mountain-tops, a tattooed and decorated member of the Iban tribe at a riverside longhouse, a bustling produce market, a beachside retreat bordering on turquoise waters, or an orang-utan sitting in a lazy pose all mark sides of the genuine adventure which awaits the traveller in East Malaysia. From shopping for exotic souvenirs and craftwork to dining in seaside restaurants to the thrill of riding in a longboat along river 'highways' deep in the forests, it is all there for the choosing.

The history of the 'White Rajah' – the lineage that commenced with adventurer James Brooke in the 1830s and lasted until the start of World War II – is still intact in Kuching, Sarawak's capital.

But away from the cities lie some natural prizes: Borneo's highest mountain (Mount Kinabalu in Sabah), its longest river (the Rejang in Sarawak), its myriad caves (including the Niah and Mulu Caves in Sarawak), and natural parks with wonderful wildlife and flora. For a change of pace, there are plenty of beaches along the southern and eastern coasts and lots of islands for snorkelling or turtle-watching.

Getting around can be a challenge. The rivers, more numerous and much longer than on the peninsula, still provide the principal way into the interior, supplemented by smaller aircraft operated by Malaysia Airlines.

Sarawak

It is just 90 minutes by air from Kuala Lumpur to Kuching, the historic capital of Malaysia's largest state – covering

---

Aborigines of Northern Borneo

These many tribes were once collectively known as Land or Sea Dayaks.

Iban, the largest indigenous group in Sarawak, dwell in longhouses along lowland river banks. They farm rice, rubber and pepper.

Melanau inhabit the coastal plain east of Kuching, where they fish and grow raw sago.

Bidayuh, the original Land Dayaks who allied with the White Rajahs of the 19th century, are longhouse dwellers of western Sarawak.

Kenyah and Kayan are two distinct tribes but often live side by side along the upper reaches of Sarawak's Baram and Rejang rivers. They farm hill rice and rubber, and rear pigs and poultry.

Punan, the last of East Malaysia's nomads, stay upriver well clear of civilisation. The men make superb weapons – machetes and blow-pipes – and the women are renowned as basket-weavers.

Kadazandusun, Sabah's biggest tribe, have adapted smoothly to urban life – and Christianity – in Kota Kinabalu. Others live on terraced hills around Mount Kinabulu.

Bajau are Muslim sailors affectionately known as 'Sea Gypsies'. Their land-lubber cousins are admired as daring cowboy cattle-breeders.

Murut are hunters in the hill country along the Sabah–Sarawak border.

124,967 sq km (48,250 sq miles). From the air you'll be able to see that Sarawak has the country's longest river, the Rejang, flowing 563km (350 miles) from the mountains on the Indonesian border to the South China Sea. The wealth of river systems among the jungle terrain provides a vital link that will transport you to the tribes of the rainforest. Between taking river cruises or treks through the rainforest of Bako National Park, you can relax at the beachside of Santubong and Damai, just 40 minutes from Kuching. In eastern Sarawak, you can pursue more strenuous but exhilarating adventures in the Niah or Mulu cave systems.

Don't be surprised if upon arrival on a domestic flight you are asked to show your passport for immigration formalities.

Kuching

Unlike the other major towns of East Malaysia – Miri, Kota Kinabalu or Sandakan – Sarawak's state capital has preserved its colonial charm, having been spared from the bombs of World War II. **Kuching** is built on a bend of the Sarawak River, 32km (20 miles) from the sea. The residence and fort built by the White Rajahs *(see page 26)* lie on the north bank, while on the southern bank is the greater part of the town, including Chinese and Indian merchants, major hotels and several colonial buildings, permanent vestiges of the past.

The colonial buildings include the **General Post Office**, noteworthy for its 1930s neoclassical design and pillars, and the **Courthouse**. The courthouse site was originally a German Lutheran mission before James Brooke, the first of the White Rajahs, turned it into a judicial administration office. In 1858 that building was demolished, making way for a second and later a third structure (the one that still stands), which was completed in 1874. State Council meetings continued to be held there until 1973. Today it houses the **Sarawak Tourism Complex**. The clock tower, whose bells still chime on the hour, was added in 1883. In front of the courthouse is the **Charles Brooke Memorial**, 6m (20ft) in height, which was built in 1924 in remembrance of the second White Rajah.

Along the **Esplanade**, north of the courthouse, is the **Square Tower**, with an information centre and multimedia theatre on its ground floor.

West of the Courthouse is **Jalan India**, a pedestrian mall marking the city's Muslim centre. Sarawak's oldest **Indian Mosque**, built in the 1850s, is here. Still further west, the **Kuching Mosque**, built in 1968 near the markets, is best seen from the other side of the river. A new mosque has also been built on the north side of the river.

The main **Central Market** is located on Jalan Gambier, near the Esplanade. Here fresh fish, poultry and vegetables are sold, as well as clothes, newspapers and CDs. Nearby are the bus terminal and taxi stand.

Kuching is cradled by a bend in the Sarawak River

Despite new high-rise constructions, the numerous traditional shophouses – both Chinese and Indian – ensure the city's former qualities are still within reach. Chinese shophouses along **Jalan Padungan**, mostly built during the rubber boom of the 1920s and 1930s, offer a variety of restaurants, coffee houses and handicraft shops.

More colourful is the **Sunday Market** on Jalan Satok at Jalan Palm, which actually starts late on Saturday and extends through Sunday morning, offering a bewildering array of items; Dayaks come to sell fruit, vegetables and handicrafts and even more exotic items from the forest, such as lizards, bats, monkeys and turtles.

East of the Courthouse, the **Tua Pek Kong Temple** and the **Chinese History Museum** are near the group of grand, five-star hotels that line the river. The temple, also known as the Siew San Teng Temple, was built in 1876 and is the oldest in Kuching; it remains an active place of worship. The nearby museum traces the long history of the Chinese in Sarawak, who lived there well before the arrival of James Brooke. Another temple is the **Kuek Seng Ong Temple**, on Lebuh Wayang, built in 1895. Finally, the **Lim Fah San Monastery Association** is located on Jalan Sampang Tua.

For a fee of 30 sen (one way), venture across the Sarawak River by *tambang* (ferry) to view the **Astana** (1870) and **Fort Margherita** (1879). The Astana (which means palace in

Catcall

The town's name is said to have been given it by James Brooke, the first White Rajah, when a cat, *kuching* in Malay, ran across the room during a conference with local chiefs. The legend has been enough to justify a whole room being given over to cats at the Sarawak Museum and a leading nightclub calling itself 'Cat City'.

Malay), was originally the Brooke family's home. It comprises three bungalows under a single roof and is built off the ground, supported by brick pillars. The building has a library and a collection of artefacts associated with the Brooke family. The ground floor was the location for many garden parties hosted by the Rajahs; it was also used as an internment centre for Japanese prisoners of war in World War II. It is now the residence of the Governor of Kuching, the Yang Di-Pertua Negeri. Set among beautiful grounds, it is, unfortunately, not open to the public.

Celebrating the city's feline name

Up the hill to the right from the Astana, the road leads to Fort Margherita, now the **Muzium Polis** (Police Museum; open Tues–Fri 10am–6pm). The white-turreted edifice was built by Sir Charles Brooke along the lines of an English medieval castle and named after his wife, Margaret. It was converted to a museum in 1971. You may need your passport to gain a free pass to enter the museum. Inside, there are displays of police weapons and simulated opium dens, plus scenes of punishments once meted out to prisoners. A skull house in the museum offers a grisly reminder of another side of Borneo's history.

Back on the south side of the river, another colonial building is the **Round Tower** on Jalan Tun Abang Haji Openg. It was originally designed as a dispensary when built in the 1880s.

Also south of the river on Jalan Tun Haji Openg is the **Sarawak Museum**, which has one of the best collections of folk art and flora and fauna in Southeast Asia. The museum is divided between the old and new wings, connected by a footbridge across the road. The former was built in 1891 and styled along the lines of a Normandy townhouse; it is devoted to Sarawak's rich history and diverse cultures. The new wing, completed in 1983, has more galleries and archaeological exhibits, including a reconstruction of early human settlements at the Niah Caves. There is a book and souvenir shop.

Within the museum's grounds there is an **Aquarium**, the **Botantic Gardens** and the **Heroes Memorial**, the latter commemorating the dead from World War II, the Emergency and the Confrontation with Indonesia. Adjacent to the new wing of the Sarawak Museum is the **Muzium Islam** (Islamic Museum).

Tribal art at Sarawak Museum

Highlights of the old wing include a reconstructed **Iban Longhouse**, complete with totem-pole, chieftains' hornbill-feather headdresses and skulls of head-hunting victims; the **Kenyah Tree of Life Mural**, repainted from one at a longhouse at Long Nawang; **Melanau dolls**, which serve as charms against disease and to lure animals to traps; beads of the **Kelabit** people; and specimens of Alfred Russel

Wallace's extensive collection of insects.

The new wing is home to galleries of **Hindu and Buddhist sculptures**; Chinese, Thai, Japanese and European **ceramics** and **brassware**; a model of the **Niah Caves** *(see page 126)*, with their birds, bats and other fauna, and Stone Age artefacts and funeral boats from the 8th century AD. A photographic history of Kuching is also rewarding.

Iban cultural dance

One gallery has become the world's first **Cat Museum**, in honour of the city's feline mascot *(see page 118)*.

Around Kuching

The fishing village and peninsula of **Santubong** is just 40 minutes from Kuching. There you will find beach resorts and cultural sights, plus opportunities for jungle trekking, bike riding and golf. **Mount Santubong** (810m/2,655 ft) peers down on **Damai**, where you will find resorts along the sandy beach. Nearby is the **Sarawak Cultural Village**, 7 hectares (17 acres) of craft demonstrations and cultural performances. Described as a 'living museum', it provides an opportunity for the traveller short on time to gain a feel for Sarawak's rich culture. Full- or half-day tours are offered, with regular shuttles available from Kuching.

There are three beach resorts and a rainforest resort at Damai, each offering a range of water sports, jungle trekking trips and cultural activities. Two of the resorts, both located at

Teluk Penyu Beach, are managed by the Holiday Inn chain and are within easy reach of the Cultural Village. Outside the village, there is access to local longhouses as well as trips to the Bako National Park, local fishing villages and nearby islands, and river cruises around the Santubong Peninsula.

In Sarawak one major centre is involved with the rehabilitation of the orang-utan. The **Matang Wildlife Centre**, 35km (22 miles) from Kuching, is to take over the role of Semengoh, which no longer maintains captive animals. At Matang, while the focus of their work is on the orang-utans, there are enclosures for Sambar deer, crocodiles, sun bears, civets and bear cats, as well as aviaries holding hornbills, sea eagles and other birdlife from Sarawak.

Bako National Park

Both **Bako National Park** and **Kubah National Park** are within easy reach of Kuching. Sarawak's oldest national park, Bako is also one of the smallest, covering just 27 sq km (10 sq miles), but it offers great opportunities to see a wide range of animal and plant life. Since the park is located just one hour (37 km/23 miles) from Kuching, the visitor has a choice between a day trip or an overnight stay; accommodation includes a resthouse, dormitories and chalets. You must first travel to Kampung Bako, where you can get a boat to transport you to the park headquarters at Telok Assam. The paunchy, long-nosed **proboscis monkey** is the major attraction, but you can also see silver leaf monkeys and long-tail

Experience longhouse life

macaques as well as mouse-deer, monitor lizards and a variety of birdlife.

At Bako there are 16 well-marked, colour-coded jungle trails with bridges over the swamps to the best spots for viewing flora and wildlife. Twelve of the trails lead off from the right of the park's headquarters, just across from the arrival jetty. The **Jalan Tanjong Sapi**, a 30-minute steep climb up to the cliff-tops overlooking the bay that fronts the park headquarters, is recommended.

> Unique to Borneo, the male proboscis monkey sports the splendid pendulous nose that gives this species its name. The male also emits a formidable honk at times of great excitement or alarm. The female's nose is an unremarkable little snub, but zoologists say that she appreciates, and is even aroused by, the male's proboscis.

On the Jalan Lintang, a small observation hide at the **Lintang Salt Lick** offers the chance to see the animals at close quarters as they drink. Besides its good hilltop view over the jungle, the **Jalan Bukit Tambi** is home to several specimens of carnivorous plants: the bladderwort, pitcher plant and sundew (Venus flytrap).

The **Jalan Telok Delima** and **Jalan Telok Paku** are the best trails for viewing the proboscis monkeys as they like to bed down in a tree near the seashore. Very often, they will have been watching you long before you spot them, and if your presence upsets them, they will just honk and disappear. While at the seashore, keep a look out for the hairy-nosed otter.

Visiting a Longhouse

The opportunity to see the tribes of Sarawak in their forest homes is a privilege not to be missed. However, tours to some longhouses have acquired the artificial character of a 'tribal theme park'. Unfortunately, as tourism rises and the popularity of such expeditions increases, it is a trend difficult to escape, the only real alternative being to travel even further into the forests at added expense. But the adoption by some villagers of Western clothing or such items as televisions and radios shouldn't put off the visitor.

On offer for the adventure traveller is a choice between a day trip, an overnight stay at a guest house near a longhouse, or a stay in a longhouse itself. Tours from Kuching usually start very early and involve a two- to five-hour road journey to the river and then a one-hour cruise by longboat. Tour operators usually have exclusive arrangements with particular longhouses.

Life in the Longhouse

A typical longhouse is a communal dwelling of perhaps 20 'apartments', attached one to the other and extended as each family adds a unit of parents with children. Erected close to the river, it is built of sturdy, axe-hewn timber, preferably Sarawak's coveted belian ironwood. The structure is raised above the ground on massive pillars – a technique evolved in the past to resist enemy attacks rather than mere river flooding.

A notched tree trunk serves as a stairway to the outer, open verandah, where the families congregate, dry their washing or lay out their fish, spices, fruit, nuts and vegetables. On the inner, closed verandah are the communal 'lounges', kept for recreation and ceremonies.

Off to the side behind partitions, family dwellings consist of bedrooms and kitchens. An attic under the roof is used for storing grain or rice. The attic sometimes doubles as a weaving room.

Modern times have brought running tap-water, electricity generators, cooking stoves, and radio and television. But people also cling to their traditions, wearing sarongs and proudly bearing hornbill tattoos on their throat and arms. Hanging from pillars and rafters are the ancestral head-hunting trophies – believed to give the clan strength and good fortune.

Melenau Tall House, Sarawak Cultural Village *(see page 121)*

The format of a visit varies, but it may include cultural performances soon after arrival for day-trippers or at the day's end as evening entertainment for those staying longer. The standard tour is an initial orientation to the longhouse, highlighting the *bilik* (apartments) as distinct from the *ruai* (communal areas). Tour groups are often greeted with *tuak*, a sweet wine made from glutinous rice, and a welcome dance. The musical and cultural performance includes a *ngajat*, a traditional Iban dance. Demonstrations of the blowpipe and cockfighting are also likely to be on the agenda.

Before you leave, your tour guide will remind you to make sure that you have gifts – cigarettes, sweets and little toys for the children – which can be bought during one of the bus stopovers earlier in the day. Malaysian tourism authorities may also be able to offer advice on reputable tour operators in Kuching who organise visits on a small scale so as not to offend tribal dignity.

Inside the Niah Caves

Tours are available to **Iban** longhouses around Kuching, and **Bidayuh** longhouses in the hill regions. Visits to the Iban are likely along the **Skrang** or **Batang Ai River**. To the east of Kuching you can visit the **Kenyah** and **Kayan** tribes. Excursions are organised either via Miri from Kuala Baram along the majestic **Baram River**, or via Sibu, from Kapit or Belaga, up the **Rejang River**. The Rejang is considered Malaysia's greatest river at some 560km (350 miles) long; a journey along it is considered one of the world's last great travel adventures. The approach to Belaga entails a passage through the Rejang's **Pelagus Rapids**. There are seven in all: *Bidai* (big mat), *Nabau* (python), *Lunggak* (dagger), *Pantu* (sago), *Sukat* (measure), *Mawang* (fruit) and, most ominously, *Rapoh* (tomb).

Niah National Park

At the **Niah Caves** visitors see the earliest traces of *homo sapiens* in Malaysia; they lived in the area up to 40,000 years ago. Later the caves were used as a burial ground, and they are now the hunting-ground of collectors of the cave-roof birds' nests. The caves and surrounding 3,149-hectare (7,775-acre) park are 480km (300 miles) up the coast from Kuching, hidden within the Miri forests.

Adventurer A. Hart Everett came across the caves in the 1870s, but it was not until 1958 that local explorer and Sarawak Museum curator Tom Harrisson made the important discovery of a human skull dating back some 37,000 years, together with 1,200-year-old red hematite rock paintings. The fragments of the Deep Skull (so-called because it was found deep within an ancient pile of bat guano), together with tools, earthenware pots, jars and later bronze jewellery found nearby are on display at the Kuching Museum.

The park, near the town of Batu Niah, is midway between the towns of **Bintulu** and **Miri**, a boomtown known for its oil exploration and extraction. The caves are accessible by road from either town, taking at least two hours from Miri and three hours from Bintulu. The park's headquarters is at **Pengkalan Batu**, and you will need to obtain a permit either here or in the town of Miri. From here, you cross the Sungei Niah (or Niah River) by *sampan*, then follow the 3-km (2-mile) plank walkway to the caves. For the cave tour, be sure to take a powerful flashlight, sturdy walking shoes with a good grip and a change of clothes – the humidity is quite intense.

First seen is the **Traders Cave**, so-called because of its role as a meeting place of bird's nest-gatherers and merchants. The main or **Great Cave** is a hollow

The original Niah people's decline is something of a mystery; their forefathers may be the nomadic Penan, who traded birds' nests and hornbill ivory for Chinese porcelain and beads.

400m (1,312ft) up in the sandstone Subis plateau. Besides giant crickets and scorpions (from which the extension of the boardwalk through the cave keeps you safe), the cave is home to millions of bats and swiftlets. The Deep Skull and other relics were discovered here.

The bats' daily droppings furnish one ton of highly valued guano fertiliser. But more lucrative than the guano are the swiftlets' edible nests – used to make bird's-nest soup – for which Chinese merchants are prepared to pay hundreds of dollars per kilo (about 100 nests), reselling them for thousands. Park authorities are increasingly concerned about the impact of the on-going harvest on the swiftlets' survival. The rush of nesting swiftlets flying into the cave at the day's end, while nocturnal bats rush past into the evening sky, is a spectacular sight.

The boardwalk continues through the Great Cave down to the **Painted Cave**, also accessible without a guide. Discovered in 1958 along with the Deep Skull, its wall-paintings

---

Bird's-Nest Soup

Descendants of the nomadic Punan tribesmen who rediscovered the Niah Caves' bird's-nest riches in the 19th century divide up the cave into jealously guarded 'stakes', handed down from father to son. To scrape the nests from the cave ceiling, the Punan climb more than 60m (200ft) up a series of swaying bamboo poles tied together, or through narrow 'chimneys' inside the rock. As the old song says, 'A lotta men did and a lotta men died' – nobody knows how many.

White-bellied swiftlets are responsible for the high-priced nests, made from pure saliva rendered particularly glutinous by a diet of algae. An inferior product is furnished by 'black-nest' swiftlets who mix feathers in with the saliva. To the dismay of Western gourmets, the Chinese insist that the viscous, translucent soup is worth the trouble.

The spectacular pinnacles on Gunung Api in Mulu National Park

representing red stick-figures of spread-eagle dancers were executed in a mixture of betel juice and lime around AD700. This cave was probably also used as a burial chamber.

Nearby are several jungle trails, with the **Jalan Bukit Kasut** and the **Jalan Madu** both clearly marked. Be on the lookout for the long-tailed macaques, together with a range of birdlife such as bulbuls, tailor birds, crested wood partridges, trogons and hornbills.

Gunung Mulu National Park

Among the largest limestone cave systems in the world, the UNESCO World Heritage Site of **Gunung Mulu National Park** (53,000 hectares/130,600 acres) is one of Sarawak's most important attractions. The cave system of 150km (94 miles) was first explored between 1976 and 1984 and requires a minimum two-day/one-night stay to be fully appreciated. The trip is demanding, and you need to be in

With permits, experienced cavers can explore Mulu's less accessible caves and wade chest-deep through underground streams. The best guides will provide miner's helmets with built-in lamps to explore the pitch-black caves. Your own equipment should include very strong shoes made of rubber rather than leather, lots of socks, tough old clothes, a pair of gloves and a light sleeping bag.

good shape, especially if you are looking to undertake the climb to the limestone-sculpted pinnacles on Gunung Api (Fire Mountain).

A 35-minute flight from **Miri** arrives at the airport near the park's headquarters. The alternative (by land and boat) also starts from Miri and is a four-stage trip. First, you travel by bus or taxi to Kuala Baram, at the mouth of the Batang Baram. From here, you take an express boat to **Marudi** before meeting up with the noon boat to **Long Terawan**, followed by a third longboat along the Sungei Tutoh and Sungei Melinau to the park's headquarters. This is the only alternative to the air trip and requires almost a full day of travel by bus and boat. The flight from Miri over rainforest in an F50 plane is considered the best way to begin your stay at Mulu and is recommended for the return journey.

There are four main 'show caves' at Mulu – Deer, Lang's, Clearwater and Wind – as well as countless other 'wild caves', which are either too dangerous or too ecologically fragile to visit without special permits and qualified guides.

To give you an idea of the vast scale of the caverns, **Sarawak Chamber**, reputed to be the largest cave in the world, is said to be capable of holding 40 jumbo jets. Tours began in 1998, but entry is usually restricted to seasoned cavers. If you wish to see this spectacular chamber, be sure to ask for details when making your arrangements.

Nearest to the park's headquarters are the **Deer Cave** and Lang's Cave. The Deer Cave, with an enormous entrance and a passage 2km (1 mile) long and up to 220m (720ft) high, was once a shelter for deer. It is uncertain whether it was also used as a human burial ground, as other caves in the system were. Like many other large, open caves, it is home to millions of bats, which fly out in a cloud at dusk in search of food. Noteworthy is 'Adam and Eve's shower', a cascade of water falling 120m (393ft) from the cave's ceiling. Deep within the cave – reached after about an hour's walking – is a hidden green valley known as the **Garden of Eden**.

Lang's Cave, nearby, was once inhabited by wild boars, and, although smaller, it has a variety of stalactites and stalagmites and spectacular rock curtains.

The Deer Cave

Both the **Clearwater** and **Wind Caves** are reached by longboat from park headquarters. The Clearwater Cave's passage extends for 50km (31 miles). After passing the moss-covered stalactites near the entrance, you'll need to have a good flashlight to hand in order to see the limestone formations. The Wind Cave is accessible to hardy cavers from near the Clearwater Cave, but other visitors must make their entry from the river.

Exploring the **Pinnacles**, 900m (2,950ft) up the side

of Mount Api, will add extra days to the tour, but there are few sights to match these gigantic stone needles thrusting like petrified hooded ghosts above the dark-green canopy of the forest. Extra time, too, is required if you wish to attempt the climb up **Mount Mulu** (2,376m/7,793ft), whose summit was successfully reached by Lord Shackelton in 1932 after earlier known attempts in the 19th century had failed. The ascent of Mount Mulu alone can take up to five days, although experienced climbers have made the journey in less than two.

The richness of the park's flora and fauna has been the topic of many scientific studies, revealing 1,500 species of flowering plants, 20,000 animal species, 8,000 varieties of fungi, 262 species of bird, 50 species of reptiles and 280 species of butterfly. Bird-life includes stork-billed kingfishers, myna birds and strawhead bulbuls.

Sabah

Covering the northern tip of Borneo, Sabah lies just clear of the cyclones that regularly sweep down across the Philippines, and so has been dubbed by generations of sailors the 'Land Below the Winds'. Its capital, Kota Kinabalu – popularly known as KK – looks out on the South China Sea, with the Sulu to the northeast and the Sulawesi seas to the south.

KK lies in the shadow of the Crocker Mountain Range, home of Mount Kinabalu, Southeast Asia's tallest mountain at 4,101m (13,455ft). The Kinabalu National Park is just one of six protected regions in the state.

The capital serves as a landing-stage for visits to an offshore national park of coral islands. On the east coast, Sandakan provides a base for visiting the Turtle Islands and the famous orang-utans of Sepilok. The visitor can choose from fishing, snorkelling, deep-sea diving, leisurely coral cruises in the beautiful waters surrounding Sabah, or just exploring KK's markets.

Kota Kinabalu

Known as Jesselton (after Sir Charles Jessel, chairman of the North Borneo Chartered Co.) until World War II, **Kota Kinabalu** was renamed Api (Fire) by the occupying Japanese. Today's KK was rebuilt from the ashes of the war after allied bombing razed the city during the Japanese occupation. KK is at present a prosperous and busy seaport, with a growing manufacturing base and a population of 400,000. Rebuilt in a modern style, it is blessed with a beautiful natural setting: tree-clad coral islands off the coast and the dramatic backdrop of Mount Kinabalu to the west. The city is generally used as a base for visiting the surrounding national parks. You'll find a **tourist information office** (a former post office) on Jalan Gaya.

White-water action

The large, golden dome of the **State Mosque**, at the corner of Jalan Tunku Abdul Rahman and Jalan Penampang, can be seen as you come into town from the airport. Nearby is the **Sabah State Museum** or Jalan Museum (open Sat– Thur). The museum is styled along the lines of Murut and Rungus longhouses, and set in grounds where you will also find a number of steam engines. Its historic photographic collection provides a chance to see the township as it was before the devastation of war.

Next door is the **Science and Technology Centre** and an **Art Gallery**. Across from the museum is an **Ethnobotanic Garden**, offering the chance to see a range of tropical plants.

One block east of Jalan Gaya is the **Atkinson Clock Tower**, built in 1905. Along with the tourist information office, it is one of the few pre-war structures still standing.

Walk up the hill to enjoy the view from the **Signal Hill Observatory**. One of the most popular markets in town is the **Jalan Gaya Street Market**, held every Sunday morning. At the waterfront can be found the **Filipino Market**, near the general and fish markets.

Malaysia is known for its great diversity of coral species

On the north side of town is the gleaming **Sabah Foundation** building, a 30-storey cylinder mounted on a polygonal pedestal, looking like a flat-topped space rocket. Construction of the tower came was financed by timber royalties to the state, after the foundation, devoted to state educational projects, was established in 1966. This tower offers a great view of the city.

The Coral Islands

Just a brief boat ride from KK are the five islands of the **Tunku Abdul Rahman Park**, which was created in 1974. Boats can be rented at the waterfront, near the Hyatt Hotel, for either a group or individual tour to the islands. All five islands lie within an 8-km (5-mile) radius and provide first-class beaches and superb opportunities for swimming and snorkelling, and there are boardwalk trails into the islands' jungle interiors.

Pulau Gaya is the largest of the coral islands. The park headquarters here can give you information about the flora and fauna, both underwater and in the forest. The sandy **Police Beach** on the north shore is good for swimming and exploring marine life among the coral reefs. On the boardwalk trail across a mangrove-swamp forest, look out for monkeys, bearded pigs and giant-beaked pied hornbills.

Some of the best nature trails are on neighbouring **Pulau Sapi**, a 10-hectare (25-acre) islet off the northwestern coast of Pulau Gaya. South of Sapi is **Pulau Manukan**, the most developed of the islands, with hilltop and beach-side chalets, a restaurant, swimming pool, and tennis and squash courts. Tiny **Pulau Mamutik**, covering just 6 hectares (15 acres) and largely unspoiled, with plenty of reefs at its northeastern end, is very popular with divers and snorkellers. The most remote and least developed island, with the park's finest coral reefs and abundant marine life, **Pulau Sulug** offers a more tranquil and deserted atmosphere.

Around Kota Kinabalu

From the bus station near Jalan Tun Razak, inexpensive journeys can be made to locations not far from the city. Visit one of the many *tamu* (village markets) held on different days of the week – ask at Kota Kinabalu's tourist information office. The best are at **Tuaran** 33km (20 miles) from KK, and further north at Kota Belud, where one finds the **Mengkabong** and **Penambawan** Bajau villages.

At Donggongon in the village of Kuai, 10km (6 miles) south of KK on Penampang River, is the Kampung Monsopiad. It was built to commemorate the legendary warrior Monsopiad, whose forte was beheading his enemies. Forty-two of his 'trophies' are on show at the **Cultural Village**.

To view the nearby tropical jungle, ride on the railway to **Beaufort**, 40km (25 miles) northwest of the town of **Tenom**, an agricultural research station. Although the train begins its journey at Tanjung Aru, you can save time by taking a taxi to Beaufort and then another from Tenom back to Kota Kinabalu. At Beaufort, Chinese shophouses stand on stilts next to the Padas River. The **North Borneo Railway**, an old-fashioned steam locomotive, runs to Papar, with lunch on board for tourists.

South from KK, heading towards the Crocker Mountain Range, is the **Rafflesia Centre**. This is dedicated to the world's largest flower, the rafflesia, of which there are 14 varieties.

Kinabalu Park

The cool, refreshing temperatures and spectacular scenery make a journey to **Kinabalu Park**, a UNESCO World Heritage Site, more than worthwhile. Even if you are not about to make the vigorous climb to the mountain's summit, the scenery, plants and wildlife close to the park's headquarters are rewarding. Looming huge and dark in the light of dawn, the peak is revealed in its full splendour. But it is often hidden as morning clouds sweep upwards once again to shroud it in mist.

At 4,101m (13,455ft), **Gunung Kinabalu** is the highest peak between the Himalayas and New Guinea. Its name means 'sacred home of the dead' to the Kadazan who dwell on its lower slopes. The park can be reached by road 90km (56 miles) from Kota Kinubalu. There is a special bus service from KK, but arrive early, as the bus departs once full. The trip to the park headquarters takes at least two hours, though only one and a half hours on return. There are also regular buses plying the highway between KK and Sandakan. The journey from Kota Kinabalu to the park and the climb up into the Crocker Range

Mt Kinabalu, the highest peak from the Himalayas to New Guinea

takes you through Malaysia's varieties of forest and landscape, from coastal mangrove to cloud forest to sub-alpine meadow.

The park covers 754 sq km (291 sq miles), with temperatures far cooler than on the coast. They ease to a gentle 20°C (68°F) at park headquarters and drop to freezing point at the lodge where climbers spend the night prior to their pre-dawn assault on the summit, so warm clothing is a must for park visitors, as well as rainproof clothing for those climbing the mountain *(see page 173)*.

To climb the summit, it is necessary to book at the **Sabah Parks Headquarters** in Kota Kinabalu well in advance, especially in the months of April, July, August and December. The climb requires two days, with an overnight stay at a chalet at the point where the climb begins. The park offers a good restaurant and a wide range of accommodation, from chalets to simple hostels. At the park's headquarters arrangements are made for your mountain guide, porters and transport to the station where the climb begins. There are multimedia and slide shows, and trail maps are available for those who want to set out on their own (but be careful, as some trails are not as well marked as others). Those with a hardy constitution may like to swim in the cool Liwago River nearby. A small but comprehensive **Mountain Garden** provides a good introduction to the plant life you will find in Kinabalu's forest.

The pride of the mountain's plant life is its 1,500 different orchids, found up to an altitude of 3,800m (12,464ft). Ferns are also present in their hundreds. Rhododendron-lovers may find 26 different varieties, together with 60 types of oak and chestnuts. But the most fascinating flora remain the pink-speckled, carnivorous pitcher plants (see below).

Many of the local forest's 100 mammals are difficult to spot; the few orang-utans, for instance, are practically invisible, but you can at least hear the gibbons whooping. Besides the usual sambar, mouse-deer, bearded pigs and clouded leopards, there are 28 species of squirrel as well as the doll-like slow loris and the tarsier. Kinabalu also has 250 species of birds, including

---

The Pitcher Plant

The pitcher plant consists of a bowl often shaped like a miniature tuba with a curved lid sticking upright when open. Why do insects fall in? Those that go for the nectar under the pitcher lid get away safely. Others going for the nectar glands under the pitcher's rim fall into a digestive liquid mixture of rainwater and enzymes. Unable to climb back up the sticky, scaly interior, they drown and are slowly digested. Cashing in on the activity around these plants, some spiders spin webs across the inside of the pitcher's mouth and catch the falling insects.

The giant of the species is the *Nepenthes rajah*, with one pitcher measuring a record 46cm (18in) and holding 4 litres (7 pints) of water. They have been found digesting frogs and even rats.

the scarlet sunbird, long-beaked spider-hunter, fork-tailed grey drongo, crested serpent eagle, white-rumped shama and laughing thrush.

Each year a marathon race – or 'Climbathon' – is held on the mountain. The record is presently held by a British man, Ian Holmes, who ran to the summit in just 2 hours, 42.07 seconds. For ordinary mortals the climb takes two days. Meals and bedding are provided at the mountain lodges for the overnight stop. Note that rates charged by the park differ between week-days and weekends. Armed with warm and rainproof clothing for the mountain

The unmistakable Donkey's Ears

mists, pocket flashlight, and a stock of bananas and chocolate for energy, you make an early morning start. After a stretch of road, the climb proper begins at **Timpohon Gate**. As you climb, you will notice the change from bamboo groves to oaks (the forest here has 40 different varieties), myrtle, laurel and moss-covered pines. The trees become more gnarled and stunted as you approach the barren granite plateau at the summit.

The first shelter at **Carson's Falls** is at 1,951m (6,400ft). The best chance to see pitcher plants on the trail is at the **Second Shelter** on the trail at 2,134m (7,000ft), but remember, no picking. You make your overnight stop at the **Laban Rata Resthouse**, or the **Panar Laban Hut**, **Waras Hut**, or **Gunting Lagadan** at 3,353m (11,000ft). *Panar Laban* means

Place of Sacrifice, and it is here that seven white chickens and seven eggs are offered by Kadazan climbers to the spirits of the sacred mountain each year.

To get to the summit at sunrise, you must get up at about 2am. You make your way up across a barren plateau of flaked and pitted granite. The **Sayat Sayat Huts**, 3,811m (12,500ft), are the last shelters before the summit. Directly to the north are the **Donkey's Ears** rocks, and behind them the **Ugly Sisters**, as you make your way west to **Low's Peak** (4,101m/13,455ft), the highest of the mountain's nine peaks. (British officer Hugh Low, a highly successful Resident in Perak, reached the summit plateau in 1851.) Even if the altitude does not take your breath away, the view from the Crocker Range and out to the Philippine Islands will. But one cannot loiter long on the summit, as it soon becomes enveloped in mid-morning mists, making the descent treacherous for even the most experienced climbers.

Poring Hot Springs

The **Poring Hot Springs**, 37km (23 miles) from the park headquarters, offer great relief to climbers after the surprisingly tough climb down the mountain. The springs, with their soothing sulphur baths, were developed by the Japanese during World War II. Cool off at the **Langanan Waterfall** along one of trails, or at the **Kepungit Waterfall**, a site rich in butterflies and bat-filled caves. Nearby are groves of towering bamboo (*poring* means bamboo in Kadazan) and there are lodgings in chalets and hostels as well as a campsite.

Sandakan

Stretched along a narrow strip of land between steep hills and the Sulu Sea, **Sandakan** is the gateway to the Turtle Islands National Park, the Gomtanong Caves and the Sepilok Orang-Utan Sanctuary. Once the capital of British North Borneo, modern Sandakan, like Kota Kinabalu, was devastated by Allied bombing and burning during World War II, leaving little evidence of the former township.

The lively **Waterfront Market** is a good starting point for the visitor. Sandakan's oldest temple, originally built in the 1880s, is dedicated to the **Goddess of Mercy**, although modernisation has detracted from its character. The ornate **Puu Jih Shih Buddhist Temple**, built for a vast sum in 1987, stands on the hilltop above Tanah Merah, south of Sandakan town. The temple is

Soaking in Poring Hot Springs

ablaze with the red and gold of dragons, gilded Buddhas and gleaming lamps and with the fragrance of burning incense.

You can also tour the home of **Agnes Keith**, an American writer whose life in Sandakan from 1932–54, including experiences in a prisoner-of-war camp, was documented in three novels, including *Land Below the Wind*. Her pre-war home was destroyed but faithfully reconstructed upon her return with her husband in 1946.

Other links to the war years include the **Australian Memorial** on the site of the former prisoner-of-war camp in Taman Rimba, off Labuk Road. It commemorates the Allied soldiers who lost their lives during the Japanese occupation and serves as a remembrance of the Death March by 2,400 soldiers – mostly Australians – from the camp to Ranau in September

1944. There is also a small Japanese graveyard in the corner of the old cemetery on the hills overlooking the town.

The Kinabatangan River Basin

The Kinabatangan Basin, some 80km (50 miles) southwest of Sandakan, offers a good opportunity to catch sight of a range of wildlife, especially elephants, hornbills, monitor lizards, macaques and orang-utans, not to mention the elusive proboscis monkey or the rare rhinoceros. The Kinabatangan is a rewarding river for wildlife enthusiasts, and trips can be organised with tour operators at Sandakan.

Another access point to the wilds of Sabah is through the **Danum Valley Conservation Area**. The valley is 80km (50 miles) inland from Lahad Datu on Sabah's east coast. Here are a range of walking trails through the protected forests, home to the western tarsier, orang-utan, leopard cat, deer, Malayan sun bear, smooth otter and 16 varieties of birdlife.

▶ The Sepilok Orang-Utan Sanctuary

A 30-minute drive west of Sandakan, this nature reserve provides a rehabilitation centre for young orang-utans, previously held in captivity, which prepares them to live in the forest unaided. Boardwalk trails and muddy paths take visitors through the forest to the feeding centres.

See orang-utans at Sepilok

These highly theatrical, russet-furred apes exist at three levels in Sepilok's rainforest: tame, entirely in the care of the zoologists; semi-tame, living within reach of the sanctuary's feeding points; and wild, having moved off to remote parts of the forest away from their prying human cousins. Many of the orang-utans are as curious as the visitors. They have flashy tastes, preferring to snatch at bright objects rather than dull ones. They also have a good sense of parody. Watching someone put up an umbrella in the rain, they will immediately mimic this, using leaves and twigs. And they show a weary disdain for the antics of photographers leaping around them.

In Malay, orang-utan means 'forest person' – an appropriate mark of respect for the mammal biologically closest to man. These intelligent, russet-coloured apes live in the swamp forests of Sabah and Sarawak. They are very individualistic nomads, meeting occasionally to share a fruit supper before going their own way. Some visitors to Sepilok confuse them with the similarly coloured red-leaf monkeys – but unlike monkeys, orang-utans have no tails.

Optimistic figures put the numbers of orang-utans at between 10,000 and 20,000 in Sabah, mostly living in swampy forest areas. While still free from being listed as endangered, fears are nevertheless held that unbridled timber-cutting could sharply reduce their numbers.

Turtle Islands Park

From July to October, green and hawksbill turtles gather to lay their eggs on the island beaches north of Sandakan Bay. The park is 40km (25 miles) from Sandakan and is comprised of three islands – **Pulau Selingaan**, **Pulau Bakkungan** and **Pulau Gulisaan** – with a total coverage of 1,740 hectares (4,295 acres). At Pulau Selingaan there are three fully-furnished chalets where up to 20 people can stay, and from which you can maintain your overnight vigil.

WHAT TO DO

Sightseeing is, of course, only a part of your visit to Malaysia. You will probably want to take time to shop for traditional arts and crafts in Kuching, check out the night markets of Kuala Lumpur, or drop by a few Chinese antiques shops in Penang. Those who wish to can have quite an active holiday just sampling the local shopping scene. And Malaysia offers a showcase of festivals of events and festivities throughout the year as well.

SHOPPING

A variety of goods are available throughout Malaysia. Large department stores and malls are to be found in most major cities, with night markets adding colour, while antiques shops brim with traditional handicrafts and Chinese antiques. *Batik* fabric designs, silver- and pewter-ware and silk brocaded *songket* cloth are popular items.

The night markets often offer items not likely to be found in the malls, especially if you are in pursuit of bootleg CDs. In Sabah, you may even be able to buy a buffalo, though shipping is not included in the purchase price. Bargaining, away from the major department stores, is required etiquette; but make sure on more expensive items that you have a good idea of retail prices before you begin.

Malaysia's tax havens are Pulau Langkawi and Labuan. Duty-free areas are also found at Rantau Panjang and Pengkalan Kubur, both in Kelantan, and Padang Besar and Bukit Kayu Hitam in Kedah. A sampling of duty-free shops can also be found at city centres and airports in Kuala Lumpur, Johor Bahru and Penang.

Top-spinning or *gasing* is a popular Malay sport

What to Buy

Most major towns have **handicraft stores** like KL's Craft Complex on Jalan Conlay, which act as a showcase for products from all over the peninsula and East Malaysia. KL's Central Market gives you a wider selection. As far as quality is concerned, some of the best traditional products are to be found in the **museum shops** in Kuala Lumpur, Melaka, Kuching and Kota Kinabalu. The selection is more comprehensive in the markets and shops of Kelantan, Terengganu, Sarawak and Sabah. In Kota Bharu or Kuala Terengganu, take a guided *kampung* tour to see the craftsmen at work – you'll often find that you can get their products at a better price than in town.

Batik: Bright and enticing, these colourfully patterned fabrics are today both hand- and factory-made in Kelantan and Terengganu, but had their origins in the Malay kingdoms of

Songket, the favoured material for royal occasions

Java more than 1,000 years ago. The technique remains the same, although it was adopted on the peninsula only in the 20th century. A design of melted wax is applied to cotton or silk, using a metal stencil. The fabric is then dipped in cool vegetable or synthetic dye, which colours the cloth around the wax pattern. The piece is then dipped in hot water to remove the wax, leaving a lighter design behind. The process may be repeated for multiple colouring. Tradi-

A Chinese painter in KL's Central Market

tionally, certain designs were reserved for royalty, but today elegant geometric or exuberant, stylised floral patterns are available to all. You can either purchase the cloth and have it tailored back home or buy a sarong – useful at the beach over a bikini. Other items include hats, scarves, ties, purses, kaftans, shirts and wall-hangings. Do note that the quality of batik can vary greatly.

Kain Songket: *Kain Songket* (silk brocade) is a speciality of Terengganu. On a hardwood frame, silver and gold threads are woven into fine silk, usually of emerald green, dark red, purple, or royal blue. Besides geometric and floral patterns, you will also find handsome fan and dagger motifs. *Songket* was originally reserved for royalty, but is today also used for bridal dresses, ceremonial robes, cushion-covers and handbags.

Silverwork and pewter: The silversmith's centuries-old skills, originally developed at the court of Perak, are contin-

A selection of Malaysian crafts

ued today in rural Kelantan. As Islam prohibits the representation of human or animal figures, the work done here is the happy result of imposing much simpler patterns than the often elaborate silverware across the border in Thailand. The work remains exquisite despite this perceived limitation. Besides earrings, brooches, necklaces and bracelets, you will find plaques and filigree jewellery, perfume bottles, snuff boxes (originally designed for betel nuts), belt buckles, caskets, lacquered trays and magnificent bowls.

Pewter-work, in the form of goblets, clocks, tankards, wine carafes, trays and salt- and pepper-shakers, is a luxury side-product of the tin industry. It is actually 95 percent tin, hardened with a 5 percent alloy of antimony and copper. The major names to look out for are Royal Selangor and Tumasek Pewter, both available throughout the country. Royal Selangor is on sale in KL at several major hotels as well as department stores. It is also made and sold in Singapore. The Tumasek Pewter factory is on Jalan Kuang Bulan in Taman Kepong.

Other craftwork: One of the most attractive products of the traditional arts is the highly decorative **puppet** used in the *wayang kulit* shadow theatre *(see page 152)*. The demons, clowns and kings that you can watch being made in a Kelantan rural workshop can make splendid ornaments.

More practical but quite decorative are bamboo and rattan **baskets** and **mats** woven from nipa palm leaves.

In **Kuching** look for Iban *pua kumbu* (hand-woven **blankets**), wooden hornbill carvings used in rituals, and silver jewellery, woven Bidayuh baskets, Orang Ulu beadwork and woodcarving, and Punan blowpipes and mats. Most antiques and curio shops are around the main bazaar just behind the Esplanade, with a few in the Padungan area.

An authentic **blowpipe** is one of the most accomplished pieces of indigenous workmanship in all of Malaysia. Really good ones are now increasingly rare and quite expensive, and their length, 2m (over 6ft), makes them difficult to carry around. Failing a real hardwood blowpipe, you can buy the handsome quiver of stout, rattan-bound bamboo with the poison darts (minus the poison), both authentic, and a shorter pipe of bamboo that does a perfectly serviceable job of blowing darts into your cork dartboard at home.

Straight and Narrow Blowpipes

Kayan, Kenyah and nomadic Punan hunters make the best *sumpitan* (blowpipes) from coveted Sarawak straight-grained hardwood. From the felled tree, they cut a piece about 2.5m (8ft) long and shave it with an adze to a cylindrical form about 10cm (4in) in diameter. This straight but rough pole is lashed firmly to a series of supports so as to stand perfectly upright. Its upper end projects above a platform where a craftsman – with a chisel-pointed iron rod as his drill – slowly and meticulously bores a dead straight hole down through the pole. The weapon's bore must be as clean and polished as that of a rifle barrel for the dart to pass through unimpeded. Its shaft is shaved, rounded and smoothed to produce a finished blowpipe of about 2½cm (1in) in diameter.

The pipe often comes with a sharp spear point at its non-blowing end to finish off larger prey such as deer, wild pig or, perhaps, in the old days, you and me, who would only be stunned by the amount of poison on the tip of the dart. The poison is made from the sap of the ipoh tree.

Avoid pointing with your fingers, which in Malay culture is considered rude. It is better to extend the flat of your hand in the direction you wish to indicate.

Sarawak **pottery** is ochre-coloured with bold geometric designs. Sayong pottery, from Perak, has a glossy black colour. There is even pottery from Johor, decorated with *batik* and gold thread, giving it a distinctive look.

Antiques: Melaka's Baba Nyonya Chinese quarter *(see page 75)* is a great place to hunt and bargain for old porcelain imported from southern China, antique silver or jade bracelets, and, if you can find a way of shipping it home, a piece of furniture from the colonial days. Penang is also popular for antiques-lovers along Jalan Pintal Tali (Rope Walk), offering porcelain-ware, chains, coins, old glass, ceiling lamps and antique clocks. Occasionally treasures can be unearthed – notably old Chinese theatrical costumes and fake jewellery – as you rummage among the piles of junk in George Town's famous flea market at Lorong Kulit.

Discount and duty-free goods: You can get good deals on **watches**, **jewellery**, major brand **sports clothes** and **jeans** in the **street markets** of Kuala Lumpur – especially around Chinatown's Jalan Petaling – and of George Town along Jalan Penang, Lebuh Campbell and Lebuh Chulia. Bargaining here is almost compulsory. The fakes are best distinguished from the genuine articles by how low a price the vendor will accept. If you find you are acquiring an incredible bargain, start asking yourself whether that is what you want to pay for a piece of counterfeit merchandise, albeit a brilliant one.

If you cannot be bothered looking for discounts, you will find several good-quality **modern shopping centres** in KL on and around Jalan Bukit Bintang, near the bigger tourist hotels.

ENTERTAINMENT

Nightlife

To cater to Western tastes, the major cities – KL, George Town, Melaka, Johor Bahru, Kuantan, Kuching and Kota Kinabalu – and the beach resorts have nightclubs and cocktail lounges with live music. The jazz and popular music scene is dominated by Filipino performers of very high quality. The singers deliver stunning carbon-copy renderings of current and past hits, while the musicians are quite brilliant in their set pieces or improvisations.

Traditional Dance and Theatre

Malaysia's traditional entertainment is more often than not a daytime affair. Tourist information offices in Kota Bharu and Kuala Terengganu can inform you about times and reserva-

Dancers from the annual Colours of Malaysia celebrations

Malaysians love cele-
brating, and with so
many different religions
– Islam, Hinduism,
Buddhism, Christianity
and aboriginal animism
– they give themselves
plenty of opportunities.
They often join in each
other's festivities,
Muslims inviting
Chinese friends to their
Hari Raya feasts to end
the fast of Ramadan,
members of all the
communities turning up
for Melaka's Christian
processions at Easter.

tions. This information can also be found at the Malaysia Tourism Office in KL.

Mak Yong dance drama: This elegant art form evolved over 400 years ago in the Malay state of Patani, now part of southern Thailand, and today is performed across the border in Kelantan. It consists of a play on one of a dozen set romantic themes, accompanied by dance, operatic singing and knockabout comic routines. The latter is accomplished by the men, while all the other performers are beautifully costumed women. The orchestra of *rebab* (bowed fiddle), *tawak-tawk* (gongs) and *gendang* (double-headed drums) plays music with a distinctly Middle Eastern flavour.

Wayang Kulit shadow theatre: The most popular form of shadow theatre is known as *Wayang Siam*. It is of Malay rather than Siamese origin, drawing on themes from the Hindu epic *Ramayana*. It dates back more than 1,000 years to when Indian merchants first brought their Hindu culture to the peninsula. The stories surrounding Prince Rama and his wife Sita involve ogres, demon-kings and monkey warriors, all represented on stage by puppets. With its customary cheerfulness, Malay culture has added a comic element absent from the high drama of the original.

The small timber and bamboo theatre is mounted on stilts, and the puppets are seen as sharply etched shadows cast on a white cotton screen by a lamp hanging from the roof of the theatre. One *dalang* (puppeteer), accompanied by a band of musicians playing oboes, drums, gongs and cymbals, acts out all the parts and produces all the different voices. He peeps from behind the screen to assess the age and sophistication of his audience and varies the play accordingly. Originally, all the brightly coloured puppets were made from cow-, buffalo-, or goat-hides, but today the minor characters are turned out in plastic and celluloid. The bright colours are said to vary the intensity of the shadows and help differentiate the characters.

SPORTS

Water Sports

Most large hotels have their own **swimming pools**, which may seem like a necessity in a hot climate. The coolest and most exhilarating swim is to be had in the natural pools of

Fishing from a *sampan*

the waterfalls of Taman Negara and Mount Kinabalu national parks. But if you prefer good sandy **beaches**, head for the East Coast. The beaches of Kelantan and Terengganu, especially the turtle beach of Rantau Abang, and further south at Johor's Desaru, haven't yet suffered too much from the industrialisation polluting the West Coast. But Tioman Island has the best of the peninsula's beaches, particularly if you like secluded coves. On the West Coast itself, your best bets are the resorts on Penang, Pangkor or Langkawi islands. In Sarawak, the best beaches are northwest of Kuching, at Damai, Santubong or Bako National Park; in Sabah, either at Kota Kinabalu's offshore islands of the Tunku Abdul Rahman Park or up at Kudat on the northernmost tip of Borneo; over on Sabah's east coast try the islands in and around Sandakan Bay.

Scuba diving among barracuda

The resorts offer excellent amenities for all types of water sports: **snorkelling**, **scuba diving**, **windsurfing**, **sailing** and **water-skiing**. Scuba divers should remember that the coral and other marine life are protected species and are not to be picked or damaged.

Other Sports

The British have left their mark; the country has more than 250 golf courses, with a choice of 9-, 18-, 27- and 54-holes. When the local course is private, as at the Royal Perak Golf Club at Ipoh, your hotel may be able to get you temporary membership if you are a member of a golf club back home. Take your card along. The most comfortable courses are in the cooler hill stations, notably Cameron Highlands and Fraser's Hill. The best of the courses is at Saujana Golf and Country Club near KL, but there are pleasant 18-hole courses on Langkawi Island as well. Golfers say that the best resort course is the Bukit Jambul Golf Club in Penang.

The national sport, **badminton**, is played wherever a net, real or makeshift, can be set up for players to thwack the shuttlecock across to each other. Many resort hotels provide proper courts.

Tennis facilities are also widely available, but the climate makes it a sport best reserved for early morning, or evenings, when the courts are floodlit. **Squash** has become a popular racket game and facilities are widely available.

Freshwater **fishing** is a delight in the mountain streams of Taman Negara and Kinabalu parks or on Lakes Chini and Kenyir. Off the East Coast, you could try **deep-sea fishing** for barracuda or shark. In all cases, enquire first at tourist information offices about the necessary fishing permits. **Hunting** licences are so restricted that it is scarcely worth the trouble for the ordinary tourist.

Traditional Malay Sports

Like the arts and crafts, ancient Malay sports and pastimes are practised almost exclusively on the East Coast, though you may also see demonstrations elsewhere at cultural centres in KL or Sarawak. The best time to see them is in the weeks following the rice harvest and during the special festivals that stage statewide contests (*see page 157*).

Kelantan and Terengganu preserve a centuries-old tradition of **flying ornamental kites** measuring 2m (6ft 6ins) across and the same from head to tail. In *kampung* workshops you can watch fantastic birds and butterflies being made of paper (and increasingly of plastic, too) drawn over strong, flexible bamboo frames. Village contests judge competitors on their most spectacular flying skills – height, dexterity and the humming sound produced by the wind through the kite-head.

Like kite flying, **top-spinning** is no mere child's game. Adults can keep a top in motion for over 50 minutes. The top looks somewhat like a discus, made of hardwood with a steel knob or spike in the centre and a lead rim. The standard size is about 23cm (9in) in diameter. It takes some six weeks to complete the construction of what is considered to be a precision instrument. Villages stage team games with the objective of keeping a top spinning for the longest time. Another derivative of the game, using a different kind of top, has for its objective knocking the opponent's top out of the spinning area.

Sepak Takraw is a kind of volleyball played with a ball made of rattan, which the players can hit with every part of their body except hands and forearms. One team has to get over the net to the other team, without being in contact with the ball more than three times on their side of the court. A three-man team scores points each time the ball hits the ground on the opponent's court or if the ball is hit out of the court.

Chinese dragons in KL

The Malay martial art **Silat** came from Sumatra some 400 years ago. It is performed with elegant stylised gestures, either as a form of wrestling, or as fencing with a sword or a traditional *kris,* known as *pencak silat.*

Calendar of Events

Check precise dates before you leave, as the timing of Malaysia's many festivals tends to vary each year according to lunar calendars.

January/February. New Year's Day is a national public holiday.

Chinese New Year begins with a family dinner, and is accompanied by red banners and lion dances in Chinatown. Festivities end on the 15th day, Chap Goh Meh. KL, Penang, Kuching and KK are the best places for watching.

Hari Raya Puasa or Aidil-Fitri celebrations mark the end of Ramadan.

Thaipusam is the Hindu festival for Lord Murugan, celebrated with a procession of penitents seeking absolution at his shrine. The biggest is from KL to the Batu Caves *(see page 51)*.

March/April. Easter: Peninsular Eurasians and indigenous Christian converts in Sarawak and Sabah celebrate with Good Friday processions, most famously the Portuguese community of Melaka at St Peter's Church.

Kelantan Kite Festival *(see page 100)*.

Chithirai Vishu (Hindu New Year), with worship and prayers.

May. Kadazan celebrate Tadau Kaamatan (Sabah Rice Harvest Festival).

Kota Belud Market Festival, with spectacular high-jinks by Bajau cowboys.

May/June. Colours of Malaysia, a national celebration of cultural diversity.

June. Gawai (Sarawak Rice Harvest Festival): Enlivened by rice wine, the Iban stage cockfighting and blowpipe contests.

Dayak Day: Bidayuh and Iban get together for palm toddy and rice wine.

Festa de San Pedoa (29 June): Boisterous Christian tribute to Peter, patron saint of fishermen, in Melaka.

July/August. Hari Raya Haji celebrates the Muslim pilgrimage season.

Festival of Hungry Ghosts: The Chinese honour their ancestors.

Hari Merdeka (National Day; 31 August) is a national public holiday.

September. Kelantan Top-Spinning Festival *(see opposite)*.

October/November. Deepavali (Hindu Festival of Lights): Major Indian celebration, with candles lit in homes, family feasts and prayers in the temple.

Prophet Mohammed's Birthday involves processions and public readings.

December. Penang Carnival: Month-long merriment in George Town.

Christmas Day: Celebrated across Malaysia as a national public holiday.

EATING OUT

A meal in Malaysia can be as varied as the ethnic mix that makes up the country. Chinese, Indian, Indonesian and Thai recipes and ingredients all make their contribution. Malay cuisine itself is often a combination of all these and other things as well.

In addition to hotel restaurants, you will find conventional restaurants in the big cities, often perched on top of sky-scrapers, offering panoramic views. Kuala Lumpur, Melaka, Ipoh and Penang's George Town all have high-quality Chinese, Indian and Malay restaurants, but few of them impose the kind of formality Westerners may experience back home. Meal times are also less rigid, especially as the popular hawkers' centres often serve meals all day long. Vegetarians need not worry: many Chinese and Indian shops sell only vegetarian food.

Food Stalls. The arena for a gastronomic adventure is the open-air food court. The stalls line both sides of a street or surround a court filled with tables, each offering different dishes of seafood, meat, chicken, vegetables, barbecue, soup, noodles or rice. Every town has its popular venues: in KL, Chinatown's Jalan Petaling; in Melaka, Glutton's Corner; in Penang, Gurney Drive; in Ipoh, Jalan Yau Tet Shin; in Kota Bharu, Jalan Padang Garong; in Kuching, Lintang Batu.

> The left hand – and left-hand side – is considered to be impolite, and for Muslims eating with the left hand is viewed as unclean. Avoid using the left hand for eating, greeting or handing anything to someone.

Find yourself a free table, note its number and begin your round of the hawkers, placing your orders. You can

Satay – the world's most popular Malay food?

watch your meal being cooked right in front of you, or simply wait for the various dishes to be brought over to you.

WHAT TO EAT

Malay Cuisine

Like Indonesian cuisine with which it shares a common tradition, Malay cooking is rice-based, but the southern Chinese influence has also made noodles very popular.

The most common Malay dish is *satay* – pieces of chicken, beef or mutton (pork being forbidden, of course) skewered and cooked over charcoal. It is served in a spicy sauce of ground peanuts, peanut oil, chillis, garlic, onion, grated pineapple, sugar and tamarind water, with slices of cucumber and glutinous rice wrapped in *ketupat* (palm leaves).

Mee rebus is a combination of noodles with beef, chicken or prawns and cubes of bean curd in a piquant brown gravy.

To say that *prawn sambal* is spicy would be an understatement. It is served with *nasi lemak* (rice steamed in coconut milk), chillis and condiments.

Tahu bakar, a soybean cake in a sweet, spicy peanut sauce with cucumber slices, is served on a nest of bean sprouts. Rice seasoned with lemon grass, chillis, ginger and soy accompanies *beef rendang*, pieces of beef marinated in coconut milk.

Otak otak is a grilled banana-leaf 'packet' of fish paste with coconut. Try *gula melaka sago* pudding with coconut milk and a syrup of palm sugar, or the colourful combination of *chendol* – coconut milk with red beans, green jelly and brown sugar.

Tropical Fruit

Malaysia may not be able to match France's 400 cheeses, but it does have 40 different kinds of bananas. The tiny ones are the sweetest, while the big green ones are used for cooking. Connoisseurs sing the praises of the three-panelled rather than the commoner four-panelled banana.

Besides the common or garden watermelon and pineapple, there are some real exotica to be discovered. The largest of all is the huge pear-shaped jack fruit, hanging directly from the tree's trunk and main branches. Nicely tart in taste, the yellow flesh has a chewy consistency.

Without its hairy red skin, the white-fleshed rambutan is almost indistinguishable in taste from the lychee – delicious. The waxy yellow-skinned carombola (starfruit) does not look like a star until you cut it in slices. It is refreshingly tangy.

Once you get past the foul smell of durian, it really is very tasty. Addicts say 'Smell? What smell?' Spiky and big as a football, its flesh is rich and creamy, best of all in its wild state in the jungle.

If you are a health nut, go for the vitamin-packed guava, green-skinned with white flesh, or papaya, green-skinned with orange pulp, or the sensual mango, growing, it seems, in a dozen different varieties in almost every Malay's back garden.

Malaysia's tropical fruit offerings include 40 kinds of banana

Chinese Cuisine

With the Chinese community so dominant in many of the towns, you will often find more Chinese than Malay restaurants and food stalls. Along with the staples of Chinese cooking, you will find a wide range of regional dishes in Malaysia.

Hokkien cooking specialises in noodles. Try *Hokkien fried mee*, moist noodles with prawn, squid, pork and vegetables. *Or chien* is a seasoned omelette with tiny oysters and spring onions. In Klang and KL, Hokkien chefs make excellent *bah kut teh*, a soup of pork ribs, garlic and herbs. *Eight-jewel chicken* or *duck*, which is stewed and boned, is stuffed with diced pork, mushrooms, dried prawns, carrots and glutinous rice. *Carrot cake* is, in fact, more of an omelette made with a grated radish that the Chinese call 'white carrot'. Other Hokkien staples are *hay cho,* deep-fried balls of prawn, mashed pork and water chestnuts; and *popiah,* a rice-flour spring roll of shredded meat, turnip, bean sprouts, bean curd, prawn and garlic.

Teochew cooking is famous for its *steamboat*, a southern Chinese version of fondue – very big on KL's Jalan Petaling. Pieces of fish and seafood, meat, chicken and vegetables are dipped by each diner into hot stock in the bubbling 'steamboat' set in the centre of the table. At the end, the stock makes an excellent soup with which to finish the meal. Teochew cuisine is light and non-greasy, based principally on seafood. The fresh fish is sweet because it is first mixed with a very light mixture of sweet berry sauce, peanuts and sesame oil. *Or leon*, a Teochew dish, is boiled, sweetened yam.

A favourite hawker-stall noodle dish is *char kway teow*, with prawns, clams, bean sprouts and eggs fried in chilli and dark soy sauce. Ipoh claims its bean sprouts and noodles are

Some of the best of Malaysia's food is served at street-side stalls

the best on the peninsula, served with boiled chicken in a clear broth.

Hainan island has contributed the great dish *Hainanese chicken rice*. The chicken is stuffed with ginger, boiled, and served in pieces with onion-flavoured rice and a special sauce of pounded chillis, lime juice and garlic. They also make a masterful *mutton soup* simmered with Chinese herbs, ginger and young bamboo shoots.

> Walk through any Malaysian town mid-morning and the most crowded eateries will usually be those serving *roti canai*, a deliciously light, flaky pancake served with dhal.

Nyonya Cuisine

This aromatic and spicy cuisine is a blend of Chinese and Malay traditions developed by descendants of the Chinese who intermarried in the Straits Settlements, Melaka and Penang. The result is a much spicier version of the many southern Chinese dishes mentioned above. Most famous in Penang is the *assam laksa*, a hot and sour fish-based noodle soup redolent of tamarind, lemon grass and curry spices.

Bubor cha cha is a coconut milk creation with pieces of yam, sweet potato, sago and coloured gelatin. The Nyonya version of *otak otak*, a fish cake wrapped in palm leaf with coconut milk, lemon grass and shallots, is grilled.

Indian Cuisine

The best Indian food stalls serve their curries, rice, fish, meat and vegetables piled high on a broad expanse of banana leaf. Indians may eat with their fingers, but you will be given a fork if you wish.

Most of Malaysia's Indian community comes from the south of the subcontinent, where the searingly hot curries are sweetened by coconut milk. Chefs in North Indian restau-

A sumptuous Malaysian spread

rants tend to use a lot of yogurt and a more subtle variety of spices. Since World War II, their numbers have been increased by Muslim immigrants from Pakistan and Bangladesh, who have added beef to the traditional mutton and chicken dishes. Many Hindu restaurants, particularly around the temples, are purely vegetarian, offering delicious variations on curried aubergine, tomatoes, potatoes, lentils and okra (lady's fingers), accompanied by traditional breads – *thusai, chapati, nan, roti canai* and, of course, *papadam.*

As universal now as Chinese food, the Indian and Indian-Muslim dishes you will come across in Malaysia include *biryani* (rice and meat, fish, or vegetables cooked together, with nuts, dried fruit and spices); *tandoori* (marinated pieces of chicken or fish baked in a clay oven); and *murtabah* (rice-dough pancakes, which are folded over chicken, beef or mutton, onion, eggs and vegetables). The latter can be a handy take-away snack but is better eaten at the table dipped in curry gravy.

Drinks

With all those exotic tropical fruits just dropping off the trees, the best drink here is a simple, fresh fruit juice – mango, lime, carombola (starfruit), watermelon, guava and pineapple being the most common. Malaysians like soy milk, often sold at markets in a balloon-like plastic bag with a straw. The cheapest local drink is coconut water, from green king coconuts.

If you want a local brew, try the potent rice wine in Sarawak and Sabah. *Tuak* is the fermentation, *lankau* the processing with yeast. The local beer is very good, but imported beers are available.

To Help You Order...

Could we have a table?	**Boleh dapatkan kami sebuah meja?**
I'd like a/an/some…	**Saya hendak…**

bread	**roti**	meat	**daging**
butter	**mentega**	menu	**menu**
cheese	**keju**	milk	**susu**
coffee	**kopi**	mineral water	**air mineral**
eggs	**telur**	potatoes	**kentang**
fish	**ikan**	rice	**nasi**
fruit	**buah**	sugar	**gula**
ice	**ais**	tea	**teh**
ice cream	**ais krim**	vegetables	**sayur**

...and Read the Menu

ais krim	ice cream	**kastad**	caramel
anggur	grapes	**karamel**	custard
ayam	chicken	**keju**	cheese
babi	pork	**limau**	lemon
bawang putih	garlic	**nasi goreng**	fried rice
bola daging	meatballs	**nenas**	pineapple
cili hijau	green pepper	**raspberi**	raspberries
hati	liver	**sayur-sayuran**	vegetables
ikan	fish	**sosej pedas**	spicy sausage
kacang	beans		
kambing	goat	**stek daging**	beefsteak

HANDY TRAVEL TIPS

An A–Z Summary of Practical Information

A

ACCOMMODATION (see also BUDGETING FOR YOUR TRIP)

In Malaysia, accommodation ranges from five-star luxurious hotels run by international chains to the adequate *rumah tumpangan* (lodging house) – usually a shophouse converted into a hotel – and the really bare A-frame beach huts that offer comfort a notch above camping. The government regulates the industry by issuing licences to operate hotels and to sell alcohol, but there is no official rating system.

Hotels. International-standard hotels can be found in the state capitals and popular holiday spots. They offer marble floors, thick-pile carpets, good service, discos, live entertainment, swimming pools and restaurants serving Western, Chinese, Japanese and local food. Posted rates can be as high as RM1,000 and above but most are around RM200–500.

Two- or three-star hotels offer the basics, which ought to be comfortable enough: most have air-conditioning, and most are safe and decent.

Budget rooms. Of late, budget rooms styled after the bed-and-breakfast concept have cropped up in KL, Melaka and Penang. These are relatively clean, though you may have to use a common toilet. Lebuh Chulia in George Town is famed as a watering hole for backpackers.

Budget chalets. Another recent development is the mushrooming of budget chalets along Malaysia's lovely beaches. These can be found in resort islands like Langkawi, Pangkor and Tioman, and along East Coast beaches like Cherating, Rantau Abang (where thousands turn up to watch giant leatherback turtles nesting from May to September) and Marang.

A bare room with a bed, clean sheets, shower and toilet will cost as little as RM30 a night. For extra money, some will include a mosquito net – a necessity for sound sleeping. In the absence of a mosquito net, the trick is to burn a mosquito coil. These are green coils that look like incense sticks, but whose rather acrid smoke deters mosquitoes. Otherwise, turn the ceiling fan to maximum. If that doesn't work, your last resort is to find air-conditioned accommodation, which will probably be more expensive.

Rest houses. These are bungalows formerly owned by English planters and civil servants, now turned into holiday homes and hotels with a colonial feel. You will find them at the hill resorts of the Cameron Highlands and Fraser's Hill and in small towns. Most are privately owned.

Youth hostels and YMCAs. Malaysia may not have an extensive network of youth hostels and YMCAs, but the few available are adequate and clean. Hostels run by the Malaysian Youth Hostels Association can be found in KL, Melaka and Port Dickson. An overnight stay in a youth hostel costs about RM20 in KL in dormitory accommodation and RM15 in Port Dickson and Melaka. Contact the Malaysian Youth Hostel Association, 21 Jalan Kg Attap, 50460 **Kuala Lumpur**, tel: (03) 2273-6870/71; e-mail: <myha@pd.jaring.my>; **Port Dickson** tel: (06) 6472-188; **Melaka** tel: (06) 282-7915.

YMCAs can be found in Kuala Lumpur, George Town and Ipoh. The YMCA in KL offers the best value for money, with single air-conditioned rooms at RM66.

Kuala Lumpur: 95 Jalan Padang Belia; tel: (03) 2274-1439.
George Town: 211 Jalan Macallister; tel: (04) 229-2349.
Ipoh: 211 Jalan Raya Musa; tel: (05) 2540-809.

Please note that hotels of all classes are usually filled during local festivals (see HOLIDAYS) and school holidays. Students go on holiday for a week in January/February, a week in March, three weeks in June, a week in August and five weeks in November/December.

AIRPORTS (see also GETTING THERE)

The major international airports are in Sepang (the 'new' KL airport), Selangor, Subang (the 'old' KL airport), Bayan Lepas in Penang, Kuching in Sarawak, Labuan Island (an offshore financial centre off Sabah), and Kota Kinabalu in Sabah. You can also fly into Malaysia via Pulau Langkawi.

The new international airport in Sepang, known as **Kuala Lumpur International Airport**, or **KLIA** (tel: 03/8777-8888; <www.jaring.my/airport>), is the latest in airport systems and design. Capable of handling up to 25 million passengers a year, it is some 75km (47 miles) from KL and connected directly to the capital by a high-speed rail link called the ERL, a 30-minute ride for RM35. Transfers are also conducted by limousine or coach. Limousines are luxurious and expensive at around RM90, but sharing is possible. Coaches, which run regularly, are RM25. A transfer to your hotel comes at an additional charge. A local taxi fare from the city to the airport is around RM65.

The journey from the city takes up to one hour even with the excellent expressway system and the vehicle travelling at the maximum 110km/h (69mph) speed limit.

Subang Airport is now largely used for private flights. Make sure you know whether your departure is from the 'new' or the 'old' airport.

Departure taxes (RM6 to domestic destinations, RM45 to everywhere else, including Singapore and Brunei) are included in your ticket price.

ALCOHOL

There is no ban on alcohol in Malaysia. However, in certain states like Kelantan, Terengganu, Perlis and Kedah, there is stricter control on the sale of alcohol outside hotels because of the stronger Islamic influence in these predominantly Malay states. Only non-Muslims are allowed to purchase alcohol from shops and restaurants.

In KL and larger cities, supermarkets and stores stop selling alcohol at 9pm. Pubs and bars serve till midnight. Discos stay open until 2am.

If you visit a Sarawak longhouse, the Ibans (natives of Sarawak) will welcome you at every doorway with a glass of *tuak*, a sweet wine made from glutinous rice. It certainly is a warm way of breaking the ice. Sabah has its own version of the potent wine, which is called *tapai*.

B

BUDGETING FOR YOUR TRIP

Travelling to Malaysia can be done on a wide range of budgets, whether you stay in a Chinese-run hotel in eastern Malaysia or a plush resort on

Langkawi Island. A well-connected bus network supplements the extensive airlinks on the peninsula. Air transport and ferry lines on Sabah and Sarawak compensate where road transport is lacking.

Accommodation. A room at an expensive (4- or 5-star) hotel will cost about RM200–500 per night; for an average (2- or 3- star) hotel, expect to pay RM100–80 per night; for an economy room (no air-conditioning, perhaps with a shared bath) expect to pay RM30–40. Rooms in East Malaysia are significantly more expensive (perhaps 50 percent more).

Meals. Food in Malaysia is relatively inexpensive, and apart from high-end restaurants, you can eat well on a very modest budget. You will pay more at fancier places in KL and Penang. A meal for two at an expensive restaurant could cost as much as RM100–200; at a moderate restaurant expect to pay RM50–100; and if you eat at an inexpensive restaurant or food court, expect to pay RM30 or less.

Internal transportation. An express train trip rarely costs more than RM100; a flight from KL to Kuching in Sarawak or Kota Kinabalu in Sabah can cost RM300–600 depending on when you fly and how far in advance you purchase your ticket.

Budget airline, Air Asia, offers a no-frills flight service at unbeatable prices to most domestic destinations. Details at <www.airasia.com>.

Sightseeing. Admission to museums is often free or at least very inexpensive (RM1–2). More costly are national parks, particularly if you need to hire guides. Entry permits may be as little as RM6 for Taman Negara (including a camera permit); a guided walk may cost RM35; a guide will cost around RM150 per day. At Mount Kinabalu, a climbing permit is RM50, with additional charges for insurance and guides. Transport will add to these charges, particularly if hiring a boat.

C

CAMPING

There is no organised system for campers but camping is a good and cheap option in Malaysia. Campsites are available within the major national parks like Lake Chini, Taman Negara (National Park) in Pahang, and the Bukit Cahaya Seri Alam park in Shah Alam, Selangor, but you have to pay to pitch your tent there. A two-person tent can be hired for RM6 per night and a four-person tent for around RM12. You have to pay RM1 to register as a camper at Taman Negara. For more information, check with local tourism authorities or national park offices in the state capitals you may be visiting. Some popular camping sites are found at:

Taman Negara, Pahang: Wildlife and National Parks Department, Km 10, Jalan Cheras, 56100 Kuala Lumpur; tel: (603) 9075-2872; e-mail: <pakp@wildlife.gov.my>; <www.wildlife.gov.my>.

Endau Rompin National Park: National Parks (Johor) Corporation, JKR 475, Bukit Timbalan, 82503 Johor Bahru, Johor; tel: (607) 223-7471; e-mail: <jnpc@johorpark.com>; <www.johorpark.com>.

CAR HIRE (see also DRIVING)

Several car hire companies, including some international names, are based in major cities and listed in the *Yellow Pages*. You will also find car hire counters at the following airports: Sepang, Subang, Penang, Ipoh, Johor Bahru, Kuantan and Kerteh. It can be difficult to hire a car in Sarawak and Sabah.

Rates range from RM150–700 daily, depending on the make and engine capacity of the car. A Proton Wira 1.3 can be hired at RM150–60 per day with unlimited mileage. A Mercedes Benz 200 will cost about RM700 per day with unlimited mileage. Major credit cards are accepted. The car will be delivered with a full tank of petrol and must be filled up before you hand it back. You need an international driving licence or a valid licence from your own country. Drivers must be over 25 years of age.

CLIMATE

Malaysia is a tropical country, and contrary to illusions created by travel brochures, the climate can be an irritant, especially if you have just departed from a country in the midst of winter. The Malaysian climate is hot, humid and wet. Daily lowland temperatures range from 21–32°C (70–90°F). Rainfall averages 250cm (98in) annually. Nights are generally cool, but afternoons are usually blazing hot.

Monsoons bring heavy rain. The northeast monsoon lasts from November until February; most affected are the east coast states of Kelantan, Terengganu and Pahang, and parts of Sabah. Due to adverse weather conditions, the National Park in peninsular Malaysia is closed from the beginning of November to the middle of January. The southwest monsoon lasts from July until September. The rain is not as heavy because of the shielding effect of the Indonesian island of Sumatra.

It is not advisable to swim in the sea or travel in small boats off the east coast during the northeast monsoon. Other than that, the seas in Malaysia are generally safe for swimming, sailing and water sports.

CLOTHING

Since the climate is hot, humid and wet, you should wear thin, light-coloured, loose clothing, preferably made of cotton. At the hill resorts, a wool sweater will suffice to keep you warm.

Malaysians dress in a relaxed manner, even at fancy restaurants. At a formal occasion, a suit and tie or a long-sleeved batik shirt will do (this garment will get you into any respectable establishment in Malaysia, including the casino in Genting Highlands). However, sandals and slippers are too casual for restaurants and discos. At the beach, anything goes except for topless or nude sunbathing. For walking around, wear a pair of rubber-soled leather shoes (as leather breathes better than man-made materials) or good canvas walking boots, and wear cotton or wool socks (since you are bound to sweat). Remember to take off your shoes before entering a place of worship. Malaysians usually take off their shoes before entering their homes. Refrain from wearing shorts or short skirts when visiting mosques and rural areas, especially in the east coast states. Clothing can be purchased for very reasonable prices, but larger sizes can be hard to find.

Dressing for the jungle. It is important to pack light when preparing to visit a rainforest, as it is more humid and you can easily get tired. Be prepared to get wet, so a light raincoat is a must. Line your backpack with a plastic bag and check that everything is waterproof, as river crossings are almost inevitable. Long-sleeved cotton shirts and cotton trousers are comfortable and will help to protect you from insects and thorny undergrowth.

If you are visiting mountain peaks, such as Mount Mulu or Mount Kinabalu, be aware that temperatures can drop to 0°C (32°F), so be sure to bring warmer clothing and even gloves. It is worth packing a water bottle, purifying tablets (or a receptacle to boil all your water), insect repellent, sunscreen, a cap, small towel or sarong and energy supplements, such as chocolate. Anti-leech socks are useful too.

CRIME AND SAFETY (see also EMERGENCIES and POLICE)

Malaysia is generally safe, but as in any other country, some basic rules apply. Petty theft occurs in tourist areas, and some consular warnings point to a high rate of credit card fraud and snatch thieves.

• Don't accept drinks from strangers.
• Don't carry too much money in your wallet.
• Don't flaunt expensive jewellery in seedy places.
• Don't leave your bags or cameras lying around unattended.
• When visiting crowded places, beware of pickpockets.
• Dress in a sensible manner.

CUSTOMS AND ENTRY REQUIREMENTS

To enter Malaysia, you need a valid passport or visa. A disembarkation card has to be filled out and handed to immigration officials on arrival. Even though Sabah and Sarawak are in the federation of Malaysia, you need a passport to visit these East Malaysian States. **Visa requirements**. British, Irish and Commonwealth citizens do not need a visa. Holders of US passports can enter Malaysia for three months without a visa.

Export of antiques and historical objects is not allowed unless an export licence is obtained from the Director General of Museums Malaysia or if the antique was originally imported and declared to Customs.

Foreign tourists must declare to Customs or the plant quarantine inspector any flowers, plants, fruit, seeds, soil samples, cultures of fungi, bacteria or viruses, and insects or any other vertebrate or invertebrate animals in their possession, as well as if they have visited any country in tropical America or the Caribbean during the previous 30 days.

Visitors entering Malaysia for more than 72 hours may purchase the following items tax-free:

• Not more than 225g of tobacco or 200 cigarettes or 50 cigars.
• Not more than one litre of wine, spirits/malt liqueur.
• Not more than three items of clothing.
• Not more than RM75-worth of food.
• Not more than one pair of shoes.
• One portable electrical and/or battery-operated appliance for personal use.
• Not more than RM200-worth of souvenirs and gifts – unless the goods are bought in Labuan, in which case the limit is RM500.
• Not more than RM200-worth of cosmetics, perfumery and soap in open containers.

Warning: The trafficking of illegal drugs is a serious offence in Malaysia, and the penalty for such an offence is death.

D

DRIVING (see also TRANSPORT)

In Malaysia, driving is on the left – a legacy of British colonialism. Road signs have been changed to Malay.

The Highway Code is of the universal type, and distances and speed limits are in kilometres. There is no fixed speed limit; it ranges from 90–110 km/h (56–68 mph) on highways and from 30–80 km/h

(18–50 mph) in urban areas and town limits. Spy cameras and radar guns are used to nab speeders. Check the speed limit signs every now and then.

Accelerated growth combined with lack of planning has led to confusing road systems in Kuala Lumpur and other major towns. After a while you'll find some sense in the confusion. Most roads are named, except for satellite towns like Petaling Jaya where numbers are used.

Roads are generally of good quality, and the new North–South Highway, which links Singapore to Thailand, is of international standard, though you have to pay a toll to use it.

E

ELECTRICITY

The voltage is 220 volts throughout Malaysia. Electricity is widely available except in remote areas and some islands where generators are used. **Note**: You will find square or round three-pin plugs in different establishments, while some old hotels use two-pin plugs. Fused adapters are easily available in department and hardware stores; they cost around RM5 each. A universal adapter is handy.

EMBASSIES AND CONSULATES

Unless otherwise noted, all are in Kuala Lumpur.

Australia	6, Jalan Yap Kwan Seng; tel: (03) 2146-5555.
Canada	17th Floor, Menara Tan & Tan, 207 Jalan Tun Razak; tel: (03) 2718-3333.
New Zealand	21st Floor, Menara IMC, No. 8, Jalan Sultan Ismail; tel: (03) 2078-2533.
UK	185, Jalan Ampang; tel: (03) 2148-2122 or 2148-2354.
US	376, Jalan Tun Razak; tel: (03) 2168-5000.

Where is the … consulate? **Dimanakah konsulat …?**

EMERGENCIES

Dial 999 if you need to contact the police, fire brigade or hospital. Major hotels offer medical services for minor ailments.

G

GAY AND LESBIAN TRAVELLERS

Homosexuality is illegal in Malaysia. Gay and lesbian Muslims, locals and visitors may be punished for sexual activity with flogging. Nevertheless, gay life is tolerated throughout the country, although discretion is advised, especially in popular meeting places where police keep a watchful eye. For further information on this subject, visit <www.utopia-asia.com/tipsmala.htm>.

GETTING THERE (see also AIRPORTS)

Flying is the most common means of getting to Malaysia, and KL, with its brand-new international airport, is the major gateway; you will sometimes find cheaper fares to Singapore or Bangkok, and from either of these gateways you can get to Malaysia by train or plane. The privatised national airline Malaysia Airlines (more widely known as MAS) flies from numerous destinations around the world. But British Airways, KLM, Qantas, Singapore Airlines and Cathay Pacific all fly to KL. Check with the closest Tourism Malaysia office, a reputable travel agent or discount company for more specific information. Many people travel to Malaysia quite economically on packages or tours.

GUIDES AND INTERPRETERS

Professional guides normally work for tour companies that organise inbound tours; few work independently. You may decide to discover Malaysia on your own, but tours or treks into the more remote parts of the country do benefit from the assistance of a guide. Most people make arrangements with tour companies in advance of their trip.

Contact a Tourism Malaysia office in your home country and they will advise on the most reputable companies. If you don't make arrangements in advance of your trip, you will find most of the tour companies in such major destinations as KL, Penang, Kuching, Kota Kinabalu and Sandakan.

Since English is widely spoken, tourists from English-speaking countries should encounter few language barriers.

H

HEALTH AND MEDICAL CARE

Most major hotels provide some medical service for minor ailments. Every town has a government hospital and major towns and cities have private clinics and hospitals. Doctors, nurses and other medical staff speak English, and chances are high that they will have obtained their qualifications from British universities.

If you have a sensitive stomach, do be cautious when ordering food and drink from hawkers' stalls. Though the tap water is chlorinated, drink boiled or bottled water. Lay off curries and spicy foods unless you're used to such exotic fare.

Pharmacies, usually located in department stores, close at 9pm.
Health regulations. A valid vaccination certificate against yellow fever is required from any traveller above one year of age who has visited a yellow fever-infected country up to six days prior to arrival in Malaysia.

If you plan to trek in the jungle, take anti-malaria pills. It is also advisable to be vaccinated against Hepatitis B or at least to have a gamma-globulin injection prior to your trip.

HOLIDAYS

Malaysia has numerous public holidays as a consequence of its varying population and their respective religious practices. These holidays are as follows:

January	New Year's Day
January/February	Chinese New Year (two days)
	Hindu festival of Thaipusam (in Perak, Penang, Selangor and Negeri Sembilan)
March/April	Good Friday (in Sabah and Sarawak)
May 1st Saturday	Labour Day
6 May	Vesak Day, a time of prayer for Buddhists
30–31 May	Kaamatan Harvest Festival in Sabah
1–2 June	Gawai Harvest Festival in Sarawak
6 June	King's Birthday
June/July	Hari Raya Haji
	First day of Muharram
31 August	National Day
August/September	Prophet Mohammed's Birthday
November	Hindu festival of Deepavali (except Sabah and Sarawak); Muslim festival of Hari Raya Aidil Fitri (two days)
December	Christmas Day

If a public holiday falls at the end or beginning of a week, many Malaysians take advantage of the long weekend to have a holiday. At such times, it can be difficult to book hotels, taxis or train, plane or bus tickets, so make sure you book well in advance.

Furthermore, Malaysians working in urban areas traditionally return to their villages (a practice called *balik kampung*) to celebrate festivals like Chinese New Year, Hari Raya Aidil Fitri and Deepavali. Try not to travel during these *balik kampung* periods.

L

LANGUAGE

Bahasa Malaysia, or Malay, is the national language. Tamil is the main Indian dialect spoken in Malaysia, and Mandarin and many Chinese dialects are also spoken. But English is widely known and used as well; there shouldn't be any communication problems unless you are in a remote area. Most signs are written in romanised Malay.

Do you speak English/ German/French?	**Boleh-kah awak bercakap bahasa Inggeris/Jerman/Perancis?**
I don't understand.	**Saya tidak faham.**
You're welcome.	**Sama-sama.**
Excuse me (I'm sorry).	**Maafkan saya.**
Help me, please.	**Tolong bantu saya.**
How are you?	**Apa khabar?**
Very well, thank you	**Sangat baik, terima kasih.**
good morning	**selamat pagi**
good evening	**selamat petang**
good night	**selamat malam**
goodbye	**selamat tinggal**
no entrance	**tidak boleh masuk**
no photos	**tidak boleh ambil gambar**
no smoking	**tidak boleh hisap rokok**
please	**tolong**
thank you	**terima kasih**
yes (correct)	**betul**
no (incorrect)	**salah**
big/small	**besar/kecil**
near/far	**dekat/jauh**
church	**gereja**
temple	**kuil**
mosque	**masjid**
palace	**istana**
park	**taman**
entrance	**masuk**
exit	**keluar**
closed	**tutup**

M

MAPS

Tourism Malaysia publishes maps of various places of interest in Malaysia. You can find these at hotels, tourist information centres, major airports and train stations. More detailed maps can be bought at petrol stations and leading bookshops.

MEDIA

Local English-language newspapers are *New Straits Times, The Malay Mail, The Star* and *The Sun,* available at all newsstands. In Sabah and Sarawak you will also find local English-language editions of *The Borneo Post* and *Sarawak Tribune.* Newsagents in leading hotels and major bookshops sell foreign newspapers at relatively high prices, often arriving very late. Special-interest magazines in English are available.

Radio broadcasts exist in Malay, Mandarin, English and Tamil. There are six TV stations: three are government-owned and the rest are privately run. Major hotels have in-house video programmes. All TV stations feature popular Western programmes in English with Malay subtitles. CNN is also aired.

MEETING PEOPLE

Malaysians are very hospitable and friendly. Say hello and they will immediately return your greeting and possibly strike up a conversation. In certain popular areas like Tioman Island, Cherating Bay in Pahang, Marang in Terengganu and Langkawi Island, many villagers have converted their homes into budget chalets, enabling the visitor to experience to some degree the Malaysian way of life. Contact the Association of Homestay Programmes; e-mail <araitu@mapro.or.ja>.

Some tour companies offer visits to Malaysian homes during festivals like the Chinese New Year and Hari Raya Aidil Fitri (a Muslim festival marking the end of Ramadan). Malaysians celebrate festivals by having open houses for neighbours, friends and relatives.

Some taboos. Malays don't like pointing or being pointed at with fore-fingers; point with your thumb instead. They also feel it is not courteous to hand over or receive things with the left hand; make it a point to use your right hand even if you are left-handed.

MONEY

The official name for the monetary unit is now ringgit Malaysia (abbreviated RM). One hundred sen make one ringgit.
Coins: 1, 5, 10, 20 and 50 sen, and RM1 coins. *Banknotes:* RM1, RM5, RM10, RM20, RM50, RM100, RM500 and RM1,000.

Keep 10-sen coins for local telephone calls. To make lots of calls, buy a telephone card. Vending machines accept 10-, 20- and 50-sen coins; some accept RM1 notes as well as RM1 coins. Parking meters accept 10-, 20- and 50-sen coins.

Banks and currency exchange. Travellers cheques are accepted at all banks. Popular credit cards can be used at major hotels, department stores and some shops. Currency can be exchanged at banks or licensed money-changers, which operate beyond banking hours (most licensed money-changers close at 8pm). Exchange rates vary, so shop around.

1	satu	20	dua puluh
2	dua	21	dua puluh satu
3	tiga	30	tiga puluh
4	empat	40	empat puluh
5	lima	50	lima puluh
6	enam	60	enam puluh
7	tujuh	70	tujuh puluh
8	lapan	80	lapan puluh
9	sembilan	90	sembilan puluh
10	sepuluh	100	seratus
11	sebelas	200	dua ratus
12	dua belas	1,000	seribu

Currency restrictions. The Malaysian government imposed currency controls in September 1999. Under the controls the Malaysian ringgit was tied to a rate of around RM3.8 to the US dollar. The restrictions required declaration of ringgit funds being brought into and taken out of Malaysia by both residents and non-residents.

In May 1999 the central bank, Bank Negara, eased the controls. Residents and non-residents will only have to declare the exact amount of ringgit they are taking into or out of the country if it exceeds RM1,000. Residents are required to declare in detail the exact amount in foreign currency they are carrying if the amount exceeds the equivalent of RM10,000, but they do not have to declare the amount of foreign currency they are holding when entering Malaysia.

Non-residents have to declare in detail foreign currencies brought into or out of Malaysia only if the amount exceeds US$2,500.

O

OPENING HOURS

Malaysia has a dual system regarding the opening hours of government offices. In the States of Kelantan, Terengganu and Kedah, the weekend is on Thursday and Friday. Government offices open Sat–Wed 8am–4.15pm, Thurs until 12.45pm. Banks open Sat–Wed 10am–3pm.

In the states of Selangor, Perak, Negeri Sembilan, Pahang, Melaka, Johor, Perlis, Penang, Sabah and Sarawak, government offices open Mon–Fri 8am–4.15pm and alternate Saturdays 8am–12.45pm. Banks open Mon–Fri 10am–3pm and alternate Saturdays 9.30–11.30am. The lunch break is longer on Friday because of prayer time for Muslims.

Generally, the private sector in Malaysia follows normal hours. Company offices open Mon–Fri 9am–5pm, Sat 9am–1pm. Post offices open Mon–Sat 8am–5pm (KL's GPO until 6pm), except in Kelantan, Kedah and Terengganu, where they close on Friday and open on Sunday.

Shops open daily until 6 or 7pm. Major department stores open until 9.30 or 10pm. Museums close at 6pm.

P

PHOTOGRAPHY

Malaysia is a photographer's paradise. From the beauty of nature deep in the jungle to white sands washed by clear seas, Malaysia offers sights that you will want to record on film.

Film and processing are relatively cheap. Processing quality has improved and shops displaying the Fotoplus sign have their equipment and chemicals checked regularly by Komal (Kodak Malaysia). Fuji is also taking steps to ensure high processing standards.

Most shops stock colour film. Slide film can be found only in leading photography shops in major towns. Also take note that not many shops sell Kodachromes or black-and-white film.

The sunlight in Malaysia can be harsh, so the best periods to take pictures are in the mornings and evenings. Furthermore, be careful with your exposure readings; overexposure is a frequent occurrence.

You can photograph anything except some Malay women on the east coast who are quite shy. Avoid taking photographs of Muslims praying in mosques. It is forbidden to take photographs in museums, art galleries, airports and military installations.

POLICE (see also CRIME AND SAFETY)

Police stations can be found in almost every city and town in Malaysia. Policemen and -women wear dark-blue uniforms.

POST OFFICES

The General Post Office in KL is open Mon–Sat 8am–6pm. On Sundays, the GPOs in KL, Penang, Johor Bahru, Ipoh, Kuantan, Melaka, Kuching and Kota Kinabalu open 10am–1pm. Post offices in other towns are open Mon–Sat 8am–5pm, except in Kelantan, Kedah and Terengganu where they close on Friday and remain open on Sunday. Stamps are only sold at post offices, but letters can be dropped into red post boxes found everywhere. Major hotels will also post your letters for you.

Malaysia has an express mail system (available at major post offices only) called *Pos Laju,* which offers delivery within 24 hours to several countries around the world.

R

RELIGION

Malaysia's traditional tolerance is accompanied by a mutual respect, which foreign visitors should also observe, most importantly with regard to taboos and dress restrictions. You should, therefore, remove your shoes on entering a mosque, or Buddhist or Hindu temple, as shoes are considered to bear the impurities of the outside world. This restriction may also apply to private homes – if you are not sure, do not be afraid to ask your host. In any case, you should not enter places of worship dressed for the beach or a nightclub. Muslims lend covering robes for women who are bare-shouldered or wearing shorts or skirts above the knees. Food taboos are less strictly imposed, but you should avoid ordering a pork dish when dining with Muslims or beef with Hindus. There is no restriction on photography at places of worship, but some may not like being photographed while praying.

T

TELEPHONES

Telephone cards are in use in Malaysia, and some public phones can be used only with such cards. Coin-operated telephones still exist, but these are for local calls only. Out-of-state calls can be made by dialling area codes or with operator assistance. International calls can be made at major hotels and at Jabatan Telekoms (Telecoms Department) offices in major cities and towns. International direct dialling, home country direct service and fax services are available at Telekoms outlets in Sepang airport. Home country direct service is also available at the KL railway station. Mobile phones are popular in Malaysia.

Here are some useful dialling codes:

International calls:	108
Long-distance domestic calls:	101
Directory assistance:	103

TIME ZONES

Malaysian time is eight hours ahead of GMT, so when it is 1pm in Kuala Lumpur, it is 5am in London, midnight in Washington, DC and Ottawa, and 3pm in Canberra.

TIPPING

Tipping is not encouraged, though some trishaw riders, taxi drivers and tourist guides may hint that they should be rewarded. At major restaurants and hotels, a 5 percent service charge is incorporated in the bill.

TOILETS

Unfortunately, public toilets are not always clean and often do not provide tissue paper; many are also in a state of disrepair. You should be prepared to use squat toilets if you are not staying in Western-style establishments. Shopping complexes in Kuala Lumpur and major towns normally charge for use of toilets (RM20–30 sen); these are much cleaner, and tissue paper is sold at the counter. Toilets at rest areas along the North–South highway provide paper, are free and generally clean.

toilets	**bilik air**
gentlemen/ladies	**lelaki/perempuan**

TOURIST INFORMATION *(Keterangan Pelancung)*

Offices of Tourism Malaysia exist in the countries listed below:

Australia

Level 2, 171 Clarence Street, Sydney, NSW 2000; tel: (02) 9299-4441/2/3.

Ground Floor, 56 William Street, Perth, WA 6000; tel: (09) 481-0400.
Canada
Malaysian Tourist Information Centre, 830 Burrard Street, Vancouver BC V6Z 1X9; tel: (604) 689-8899; toll-free 1-888-689-6872.
Great Britain
57 Trafalgar Square, London WC2N 5DU; tel: (044) 20 7930-7932.
US
• 818 West Seventh Street, Suite 970, Los Angeles, CA 90017; tel: (213) 689-9702; toll-free 1-336-6842.
• 120 East 56th Street, Suite 810, New York, NY 10022; tel: (212) 745-1114/5; toll-free 1-800-558-6787.
• **Embassy of Malaysia**: 3516 International Court, NW, Washington DC 20008; tel: (202) 572-9700

In Malaysia, there are several tourist information offices:
Kuala Lumpur
Level 2, Menara Dato Onn, Putra World Trade Centre, Jalan Tun Ismail 50480, Kuala Lumpur; tel: (03) 2693-5188.
Sabah
Ground Floor, Uni. Asia Building, No. 1, Jalan Sagunting, 88000 Kota Kinabalu; tel: (088) 248-698/242-064/ 211-732.
Sarawak
31 Jalan Masjid (just down from the new wing of the Sarawak Museum), Kuching; tel: (082) 410-944/2.

In KL, the Malaysia Tourism Centre on **Jalan Ampang** has information on all places of interest, and you can make bus, air, tour and hotel bookings. Cultural shows are held regularly; tel: (03) 2164-3929.

TRANSPORT (see also DRIVING)

By car. Roads are generally good except in parts of Sabah and Sarawak. The new North–South highway that links Singapore to south Thailand has made travelling by road much easier and faster.

By train. The KTM *(Keretapi Tanah Melayu)* offers an efficient rail service across the country, and fares are reasonable, too. A railway line runs the whole length of peninsular Malaysia and links Thailand to Singapore. Another line links Gemas to Tumpat in the northeastern state of Kelantan. In Sabah, there is a railway line that links Kota Kinabalu to Tenom. The Kuala Lumpur to Singapore service is often fully booked. There is also a new electric train service covering routes from Rawang to Seremban, with a feeder line from Kuala Lumpur to Klang.

By bus. Buses also ply the main towns. There are several companies, and tickets can be purchased at the generally very busy bus stations. It is best to book a day ahead. Give yourself 15 to 20 minutes before the scheduled departure, but don't be surprised if the bus leaves a little late. In remote places, the service is not regular and it is better to use taxis.

Mini-bus services are also available between popular destinations, such as Kota Kinabalu and the Kinabalu National Park Headquarters, for example, and the fares are quite reasonable (only RM10 for that particular route).

Intra-city travel is cheap and convenient as major towns in Malaysia are connected by buses and air-conditioned express coaches.

By plane. Malaysian Airlines (mas), Berjaya Air and Air Asia operate an extensive network of domestic flights to all major towns in Malaysia, as well as to more remote places in Sabah and Sarawak.

By boat. Though a bridge now connects Penang island to the mainland, the quaint ferry service is still in operation and offers a much more colourful and enjoyable way to reach the island. There are also regular ferry services from Lumut to the resort island of Pangkor, from Kuala Perlis and Kuala Kedah to the holiday destination of Langkawi, from Mersing to the lovely Tioman Island and nearby isles, from Kuala Besut to the Perhentian and Redang islands, from Kota Kinabalu to Labuan, and from Marang to Kapas Island.

Local transport. No city in Malaysia has an underground train system. Cities and towns are serviced by buses. A Light Rail Transport system is now operating in KL. Taxis, mostly air-conditioned, are readily available and fares are metered, though in some places, like Penang, cabbies do not use the meter. This is mostly due to a lack of enforcement by the authorities. In such places, negotiate the fare before boarding. In cities, taxis can be found at taxi stands or flagged down anywhere.

In the East Coast towns of Kuala Terengganu and Kota Bharu, trishaws are a popular mode of transport. Sometimes gaudily decorated, they make for good photos. West Coast towns like George Town in Penang and Melaka also have trishaws. Rides within town limits should not cost more than RM3, but you should agree a price before setting off.

W

WATER

Tap water is treated with fluoride and is safe for drinking. As a precaution, drink boiled water, especially in rural areas. Mineral water can be purchased in major towns.

WEBSITES

News:
• *The Star* newspaper: <www.thestar.com.my>
Tourism:
• AllMalaysia.Info <www.allmalaysia.info>
• Tourism Malaysia: <www.tourism.gov.my>
• Sarawak Tourism: <www.sarawaktourism.com>
• Sabah Tourism: <www.sabahtourism.com>
Travel:
• Kuala Lumpur International Airport: <www.klia.com.my>

WEIGHTS AND MEASURES

Malaysia uses the metric system.

INDEX